Mexican Muralist

South Huntington Public Library
145 Pidgeon Hill Road
Huntington Station, NY 11746

Influential Latinos

DIEGO RIVERA

Mexican Muralist

Mariana Medina
and Laura Baskes Litwin

Enslow Publishing
101 W. 23rd Street
Suite 240
New York, NY 10011
USA

enslow.com

Published in 2016 by Enslow Publishing, LLC
101 W. 23rd Street, Suite 240, New York, NY 10011

Copyright © 2016 by Laura Baskes Litwin

Enslow Publishing materials copyright © 2016 by Enslow Publishing, LLC

All rights reserved.

No part of this book may be reproduced by any means without the written permission of the publisher.

Library of Congress Cataloging-in-Publication Data

Medina, Mariana, author.
 Diego Rivera : Mexican muralist / Mariana Medina and Laura Baskes Litwin.
     pages cm. — (Influential Latinos)
 Includes bibliographical references and index.
 Summary: "Discusses the life and work of Diego Rivera"-- Provided by publisher.
 ISBN 978-0-7660-6991-6
 1. Rivera, Diego, 1886-1957—Juvenile literature. 2. Muralists—Mexico—Biography—Juvenile literature. 3. Painters—Mexico—Biography—Juvenile literature. I. Litwin, Laura Baskes, author. II. Title.
 ND259.R5M38 2015
 759.972—dc23
 [B]
                                    2015012777

Printed in the United States of America

To Our Readers: We have done our best to make sure all Web site addresses in this book were active and appropriate when we went to press. However, the author and the publisher have no control over and assume no liability for the material available on those Web sites or on any Web sites they may link to. Any comments or suggestions can be sent by e-mail to customerservice@enslow.com.

Portions of this book originally appeared in the book *Diego Rivera: Legendary Mexican Painter.*

Photo Credits: © 2015 Banco de México Diego Rivera Frida Kahlo Museums Trust, Mexico, D.F. / Artists Rights Society (ARS), New York, pp. 38 (retrieved from Fine Art Images/SuperStock), 45 (retrieved from Zapatista Landscape - The Guerilla, 1915 (oil on canvas), Rivera, Diego (1886-1957)/ Museo de Arte Moderno, Mexico City, Mexico/Bridgeman Images), 48 (retrieved from Iberfoto/ SuperStock); ALBERTO PIZZOLI/AFP/Getty Images, p. 18; © AP Images, pp. 56, 74, 86, 104; David Bank/AWL Images/Getty Images, p. 95; DEA PICTURE LIBRARY/DeAgostini/Getty Images, p. 26; Ed Clark/The LIFE Images Collection/Getty Images, p. 3; FPG/Archive Photos/Getty Images, p. 50; gary yim/Shutterstock.com, p. 16; GDA via AP Images, p. 32; George Strock/The LIFE Picture Collection/Getty Images, p. 9; Hulton Archive/Archive Photos/Getty Images, p. 82; Hulton Archive/ Getty Images, p. 36; Ivan Dmitri/Michael Ochs Archives/Getty Images, p. 6; Keystone-France/Gamma-Keystone via Getty Images, pp. 69, 79, 84; Library of Congress, Prints & Photographs Division, Carl Van Vechten Collection [LC-USZ62-42516], p. 65; Lucio Ruiz Pastor/age fotostock/SuperStock, p. 71; LUIS ACOSTA/AFP/Getty Images, p. 108; Marc DEVILLE/Gamma-Rapho via Getty Images, p. 112; NY Daily News Archive via Getty Images, p. 12; Peter Stackpole/The LIFE Picture Collection/Getty Images, p. 90; Photo12/UIG via Getty Images, p. 60; PSHAW-PHOTO/Shutterstock.com, p. 98; Thelmadatter/Wikimedia Commons/DiegoRiveraTombFrontDoloresDF.JPG/CC BY-SA 3.0/ GNU Free Documentation License, p. 106; Wallace Marly/Hulton Archive/Getty Images, p. 93.

Cover Credits: Ed Clark/The LIFE Images Collection/Getty Images (Diego Rivera).

Contents

1. **A Controversial Mural** 7
2. **Diego Rivera's Early Years** 15
3. **Leaving Mexico for Europe** 27
4. **Embracing Cubism** 39
5. **Rivera's First Murals** 51
6. **Diego and Frida** 63
7. **American Commissions** 75
8. **A Return to Mexico** 87
9. **Later Works** 99
10. **Diego Rivera's Legacy** 109

Chronology 114

Chapter Notes 117

Glossary 123

Further Reading 124

Index 125

Mexican painter Diego Rivera's murals promoted social change in Mexico and around the world.

Chapter 1

A Controversial Mural

Late one night in mid-April 1933, a hulking man perched on a wooden platform thirty feet in the air. The man was Mexican artist Diego Rivera, and he had a deadline fast approaching. Rivera had promised one of the richest and most powerful men in the United States that he would finish this painting in two weeks' time.

The painting in question was a large mural on the wall of the entrance lobby of the new RCA Building in New York City. Though the country was in the midst of the worst economic depression in its history, this seventy-story skyscraper had just been built by the Rockefellers, the family that founded Standard Oil Company and made billions of dollars.

The Rockefeller Family Fortune

John D. Rockefeller owned the most famous business empire of the late nineteenth century. The Standard Oil Company was founded shortly after the Civil War. It soon became so successful and powerful in the oil industry that it put all its rivals out of business. The company became a monopoly, a business with total control over a market or product. Rockefeller was targeted as a symbol of capitalist greed and cutthroat competition. To counter the strong public criticism, the Rockefeller family began supporting the arts and giving away large amounts of money to charity.

Rockefeller Commissions Rivera

At that time, Diego Rivera was the most famous muralist in the world. His work could be seen on the walls of all the most important buildings in his native Mexico. He had recently painted the San Francisco Stock Exchange and had just returned from Detroit, Michigan, where he had painted twenty-seven murals for the Ford Motor Company.

Now Rivera had been hired by Nelson Rockefeller, the grandson of the oil tycoon. Rockefeller wanted Rivera to paint a mural called *Man at the Crossroads Looking with Hope and High Vision to the Choosing of a New and Better Future.*

After six weeks of work, the mural was progressing to Rivera's satisfaction. He had painted a number of

A Controversial Mural

Nelson A. Rockefeller commissioned Rivera to paint the mural that would be embroiled in controversy.

overlapping scenes representing the fields of science, politics, and entertainment. As usual, Rivera's colors were very intense and his figures included everyday workers standing alongside world leaders.

It was the inclusion of one of these world leaders that was about to get Rivera in trouble. He painted into the mural a portrait of Vladimir Lenin, the leader of the 1917 Communist revolution in Russia. To Rivera, who believed in Communism, Lenin was a hero. To the Rockefellers, who were champions of capitalism, Lenin was a villain.

Lenin had not appeared in Rivera's original sketch for the mural, which had been approved by Nelson Rockefeller. Rockefeller first became aware of the change when a reporter from the *New York World-Telegram* published an article with the headline "Rivera Paints Scenes of Communist Activity."[1] Rockefeller immediately asked Rivera to remove the Russian leader's picture from the mural.

A Battle Over Art

Never one to shy away from controversy, Rivera refused to make any changes to his mural. He told Rockefeller that an artist had the right to choose the images represented in his artwork. Rivera's assistants working on the mural not only agreed with him, they threatened to walk off the job if he complied with Rockefeller's demand.

Nelson Rockefeller was not an opponent to be treated lightly. Overnight, the lobby of the RCA Building became an armed fortress. The entrance was blocked off,

A Controversial Mural

with patrolmen on horseback standing guard outside. Police carrying billy clubs were sent inside to surround the mural. Rivera was ordered to stop painting. One of Rivera's assistants hid a camera in her coat and quickly took some pictures of the painting. In light of what was soon to happen, these photographs would prove priceless.

The mural was hidden behind a large canvas screen. On May 9, a building manager gave Rivera a check for the balance of his fee and officially told him he was fired. Three days later, Rivera was also fired from another job—one he had not even started. Slated to paint a mural for the General Motors Building at the Chicago World's Fair, Rivera received a telegram canceling his commission. If the Rockefellers were displeased with his work, no other businessmen would risk hiring him.

In the weeks following, many artists, intellectuals, and other angry citizens staged loud protests outside the RCA Building to show their support for Rivera. Some of these demonstrators argued that Rivera's artistic rights were being censored. Other protestors were Communists who agreed with Rivera's politics. Rivera pleaded his own case at rallies and in the newspapers.

In July, with the money he had received from the Rockefeller commission, Rivera paid for the materials and assistants needed to paint a series of small murals at a school in New York City. All the time he was working, he fretted over what was going to happen to the mural he had been forced to abandon. Rockefeller had assured the

Diego Rivera: Mexican Muralist

Rivera was forced to abandon the mural because Rockefeller objected to its inclusion of Soviet leader Vladimir Lenin.

newspapers that while the mural would be kept hidden from public view, it would remain safe.

The new Museum of Modern Art offered to pay for the removal of the mural from the walls of the RCA Building. The museum curators wanted to preserve the work and display it at their museum.

A Question of Ownership

Yet on February 10, 1934, in what would become one of the greatest scandals of twentieth-century art, Diego Rivera's mural was smashed to pieces. At midnight on a Saturday, when they would be least likely to encounter protesters, workers employed by the Rockefeller organization took hammers and axes to Rivera's mural.

As word of the mural's destruction spread, many people were outraged. They viewed it as a horrendous act of vandalism. Rivera was angry at the waste of his effort, and deeply frustrated by what he saw as censorship of his artwork by a powerful businessman.

Rivera had earlier offered this perspective on a radio talk show:

> *Let us take, as an example, an American millionaire who buys the Sistine Chapel, which contains the work of Michelangelo. Would that millionaire have the right to destroy the Sistine Chapel? In human creation there is something which belongs to humanity at large, and no individual owner has the right to destroy it or keep it solely for his own enjoyment.*[2]

Diego Rivera spent his entire adult life making art for the people. He chose to paint murals in public spaces because he wanted to serve the greater public and not just the wealthy individuals who could afford to buy his work. Rivera's life was a colossal blend of creativity and passion. From early childhood he knew that the only thing he wanted to do was make art. He set out to be an artist, and he never changed paths.

Chapter 2
Diego Rivera's Early Years

On December 8, 1886 Mexico celebrated the annual Feast of the Immaculate Conception, with parades, loud music, and dancing. Into this chaotic air of festivity, Diego Rivera was born. It was a fitting coincidence for a man who himself would be outspoke, chaotic, and larger than life.

Diego was followed minutes later by a twin, brother Carlos. And not long after, their mother, who had lost a lot of blood during childbirth, fell into a coma, and was pronounced dead. The joy that her husband, also named Diego, had felt at the birth of his sons was crushed by the agony of losing his wife. Fortunately, his torment ended minutes later when his wife's maid noticed that Señora Rivera was in fact still breathing and very much alive.[1]

That María Rivera survived and had produced not one, but two sons was a reason for great happiness. The Riveras had already endured the loss of three babies

Diego Rivera: Mexican Muralist

Diego Rivera was born into a comfortable family in Guanajuato, Mexico. A modern view of the city is shown here.

at birth. Diego was named after his father and christened Diego María de la Concepción Juan Nepomuceno Estanislao de Rivera y Barrientos Acosta y Rodriguez.

Diego's father was known as Don Diego. The eldest of nine children, he had left home as a teen to join the Mexican army and fight against the occupying forces of Napoleon III of France. When his military stint ended, Don Diego Rivera invested in a silver mine that ended up failing to produce any silver. He decided to become a teacher instead and wrote a textbook on Spanish grammar. He was hired at an elementary school and immediately fell in love with the principal's daughter.

This eighteen-year-old girl was named María del Pilar Barrientos. Raised by broad-minded parents, María had been home-schooled by tutors and also studied music. María and Don Diego married and lived in the city of Guanajuato, the capital of the central Mexican state of the same name. The mountains of Guanajuato had been famous for centuries for the silver they produced.

The Rivera Family

The Riveras lived in a comfortable, three-story stone house on a hill in the center of the city. María Rivera's sister, Cesárea, and her aunt Vicenta lived with them. Mrs. Rivera had a maid, Marta, and after the twins were born, two nurses came to help her as well. A groom maintained the horse and carriage. The Rivera household was a lively one.

When the twins were eighteen months old, Carlos died. He had been a sickly baby since birth. Mrs. Rivera was so distraught at his death that for days she refused to leave the churchyard where Carlos was buried. Mr. Rivera was forced to rent a room for her in the home of the cemetery's caretaker. The family doctor advised that a major life change was needed for Mrs. Rivera to recover from her grief. She decided to study obstetrics, the field of medicine concerned with pregnancy and delivering babies. María Rivera became one of the first women in Mexico to graduate from medical school as an obstetrician.[2]

For the two years his mother was in school, Diego was sent to live for extended periods at the home of his nurse, Antonia. She lived in a small village in the Sierra Madres. Diego, who was only a toddler, formed a strong attachment to his caregiver and would later claim that he had always loved her more than he loved his mother.[3]

Possessed by the Devil

When Diego was four, his sister María was born, and he began to spend more time at home in Guanajuato. He now came more under the influence of his father and less of his nurse. Don Diego had strong feelings against the Catholic Church and had forbidden Diego's mother and his aunts, who were very religious, from taking his son to church. One morning, when Diego was six years old, the women defied his orders.

From the first moment, Diego did not like it: "On entering the church, my revulsion was so great that I still get a sick feeling in my stomach when I recall it. . . It was a mixture of indignation and an impulse to

Diego Rivera's Early Years

Rivera had a strong reaction against the Catholic church from the time he was a young boy.

laugh at the people around me."[4] The young boy got so riled up that he even threatened the priest with a large candlestick. At this, the priest declared that Diego was possessed by the devil.

This was a grave event for the Rivera family. The Catholic Church had a powerful hold on most Mexicans. The god-fearing churchgoers in Guanajuato strongly disapproved of Mr. Rivera's beliefs and the behavior of his son. From this time on, the family was made to feel unwelcome in their community.[5]

Don Diego's Influence

In addition to teaching, Don Diego Rivera served on the Guanajuato city council and was employed as an inspector of rural state schools. These schools were notoriously bad; at this time only 15 percent of all Mexicans could read. Don Diego also wrote for a weekly newspaper called *The Democrat*. He used his column in the paper to fight for changes in the schools and elsewhere. As his son reported years later, "Never a man to hold his tongue, he gave vent to his feelings. . . . In impassioned articles, he took the side of the oppressed—the miners and the peasants."[6]

Don Diego taught his son to read and encouraged his curiosity about how things worked. He bought Diego mechanical toys and brought him to the new railway depot to see the trains up close. Diego was fascinated and decided, at age six, that he wanted to be an engineer when he grew up.

Diego Rivera's Early Years

Most significantly, Don Diego advanced his son's early interest in making art. The artist later wrote:

> As far back as I can remember, I was drawing. Almost as soon as my fat baby fingers could grasp a pencil, I was marking up walls, doors, and furniture. To avoid mutilation of his entire house, my father set aside a special room where I was allowed to write on anything I wished. This first "studio" of mine had black canvas on all the walls and on the floor. Here I made my earliest murals.[7]

Mexican Mummies

In Guanajuato, the biggest tourist attraction today is a museum with a permanent exhibit of more than one hundred mummies. A rare combination of soil and climate conditions naturally preserves the corpses buried here. Cemetery workers discovered this fact when digging up the remains of people from families too poor to pay for the upkeep of their gravesites. The mummies are displayed behind glass; some are sitting, some lying down. Many are still wearing the burial clothes their families chose for them and are surrounded by dolls or photographs that had been placed in their coffins.

Move to Mexico City

Soon Diego's life became a bit more complicated. The Riveras often did not have enough money to pay their bills. Making matters worse, they had continued to feel the ill will of their neighbors. One day, in a panic, Diego's mother sold all the furniture and fled with the children by train to Mexico City. Mr. Rivera was away inspecting a school and returned home to nothing but a note asking him to sell the house and join his family.

The quiet cobblestoned streets of Guanajuato gave way to the bustling boulevards of Mexico City. The Riveras moved to an apartment that was no match for the airy home they had left behind. The neighborhood, while centrally located, was infamous for its rat population. Diego became sick, first with scarlet fever and then typhoid. María Rivera gave birth to another son, who lived only a week.

Yet the family persevered. Don Diego Rivera found work as a public health inspector, and María Rivera opened a clinic for pregnant women. At age nine, Diego began school. For two years he unhappily attended Catholic schools at his mother's urging. Though the home-schooling supervised by his father had permitted Diego to skip three grades, he was not interested in arithmetic, Bible studies, or penmanship.

Success in School

What interested Diego was art. He persuaded his parents to let him take evening classes nearby at the San Carlos Academy of Fine Arts. Don Diego tried to enroll his son in a military school for the daytime hours. It became clear at once that while Diego could draw inspired battle scenes, he had neither the physical strength nor the discipline required of a soldier.

DIEGO RIVERA'S EARLY YEARS

Based on the sketches he had been doing since he was a little boy, Diego was admitted to San Carlos as a full-time day student. The San Carlos Academy, one of the foremost schools in the country, provided both a fine arts and academic curriculum. Diego began studio classes in drawing and painting, but was required also to study math, science, and history.

The school used traditional European teaching techniques, which meant that art students spent much of their time copying the works of European old masters, artists like the French painter Jean-Auguste-Dominique Ingres. Three teachers particularly influenced Diego: Santiago Rebull taught him the "laws of proportion and harmony"; Felix Parra introduced Diego to the art of the early Mexican civilizations; and José María Velasco, one of Mexico's finest painters, taught Diego perspective—how to make objects on a flat painted surface look three-dimensional.[8]

At eleven years old, Diego was among the youngest of his classmates. One of his fellow students recalled that "Rivera came to school in short pants and shocking-pink socks, his pockets stuffed with fearful boyish things—bent pins, odd bits of string, and earthworms that wriggled freely."[9]

For the first time Diego was happy in school, describing himself later as "a model student, industrious and obedient. Determined to learn all that tradition could teach me, I accepted whatever the teachers prescribed.

Diego Rivera: Mexican Muralist

My hard work earned me the highest grades and every possible prize."[10]

One important artistic influence on Diego came from outside school. The hugely popular cartoonist José Guadalupe Posada had his studio near San Carlos. As he walked to and from classes, Diego would watch the artist at work. Posada's cartoons, printed on sheets of colored tissue paper and sold for mere pennies, depicted the lives of ordinary Mexicans. Diego would later write that it was Posada "who revealed to me the inherent beauty in the Mexican people, their struggle and aspirations."[11]

Dr. Atl

When he was eighteen, Diego won a drawing competition and graduated from San Carlos with honors. His artwork earned him a scholarship, sponsored by the Mexican government, to study in Europe. Following the completion of his high school level exams, Diego had six months before his scholarship began. In 1906, Mexico City was an exciting place for a young man with some free time on his hands.

With a group of like-minded friends, both artists and writers, Diego spent many of his days and nights in cafés and bars. The young people were often joined by a teacher from San Carlos originally named Gerardo Murillo, who was now going by the alias of "Dr. Atl." *Atl* was a Mexican Indian word for "water". The professor took *atl* as his name to show his Indian origins. Dr. Atl had recently returned from Europe excited by the new modern art being created there. While an eye injury had hampered his own successful painting career, he was trying to stir things up at the traditional Mexican academy and inspire students to learn from the new "moderns."[12]

Diego's scholarship would cover his living expenses in Europe, but he needed to raise the money himself to travel there. Dr. Atl arranged for an exhibition and sale of a dozen of Diego's paintings. The show was very successful and provided Diego with the funds he needed. Dr. Atl then not only refused to take the normal fee for preparing the show, he even added some of his own money to the total.

As an additional act of kindness, Dr. Atl gave Diego a letter to serve as an introduction to the Spanish painter and poet Eduardo Chicharro. Though he had been uncertain where in Europe to go first, Diego now had a destination in mind: Madrid, Spain.

Diego Rivera: Mexican Muralist

The Mexican people suffered under the dictatorship of Porfirio Díaz. These injustices would inspire Diego Rivera's art.

Chapter 3
Leaving Mexico for Europe

For more than thirty years, Mexico was ruled by the ruthless and violent dictator Porfirio Díaz. The period of his reign is known as the "Porfiriato" in Mexico. These were the conditions under which Diego Rivera came to adulthood.

Under Porfirio Díaz, the poor of Mexico lived in misery while the rich lived like kings. In fact, in Mexico during the Porfiriato, the rich lived like French kings because Díaz believed French culture was superior to Mexican culture. Under his influence, Mexico City began to look like Paris. Restaurants served French food, department stores sold French imports, theaters played French music and drama, and public buildings were redesigned to imitate their French counterparts. Wealthy Mexican families sent for French governesses to educate their children. Bastille Day, France's independence day, was celebrated in Mexico City as a major holiday every July 14.

The poor in the capital city had little reason to celebrate. They lived amidst filth and disease, without fresh water, electricity, or plumbing. Fully half of all infants born died before their first birthday. In the countryside, things were no better. President Díaz passed laws that made it possible for his supporters to take the lands that had belonged to generations of native peasant farmers. These powerful new landowners created huge ranches called *haciendas*. The native farmers were forced to work the land for the hacienda owners at very low wages.

On to Spain

In the cafés in which he spent the months following his graduation, Diego Rivera listened to Dr. Atl speak out against the unfairness of the Porfirian dictatorship and the importance of reviving a Mexico that was truly Mexican, and not French, in spirit. Dr. Atl encouraged Rivera to pay close attention to what was happening in Europe and to bring home a new artistic vision for his country.[1]

In late December 1906, Rivera sailed from Veracruz, on the Gulf of Mexico, and arrived in Spain two weeks later. It was his first time outside Mexico. By his own admission, Rivera was an unusual-looking traveler: "I was twenty years old, over six feet tall, and weighed three hundred pounds."[2]

Diego Rivera: Mexican Muralist

Rivera fell in love with Angelina Beloff during his time abroad. The older Beloff taught Rivera about the inequities of the world.

Leaving Mexico for Europe

When classes let out for the summer, Rivera decided to do some traveling. To save money on hotel rooms, he slept on trains and in station waiting rooms. In a waiting room in Brussels, Belgium, he bumped into his friend from Madrid, María Blanchard, and a Russian friend of hers named Angelina Beloff.

Angelina Beloff was an artist from St. Petersburg. Her parents had just died, leaving her with a small amount of money. She was taking classes in Paris and had studied with the great painter Paul Cézanne. She was pretty and talented and Rivera fell in love with her. His only problem was figuring out how to tell her. Beloff spoke French and Russian, and Rivera knew only Spanish.

Rivera and Beloff and three others, including María Blanchard, decided to see London before classes began again. They crossed the English Channel and spent a month in the huge city. Rivera had never before seen factories like those in London, and he was fascinated by them.[7]

In London, Rivera was struck for the first time by the horrors of poverty. Of course, he had seen the hungry begging in Mexico City. The difference now was Angelina Beloff. Seven years older than Rivera, she was far more aware of the world and its inequities. Before, Rivera had rarely considered the world outside the artist's studio. Despite the language barrier, Beloff made Rivera look beyond his own world for the first time.[8]

It was in the sculpture room of the British Museum that Rivera finally worked up the courage to tell Angelina

show the scholarship committee that he was not wasting its money. But Rivera also was a young man enjoying life on his own. "Towards the end of my stay in Spain," he later recalled, "I became so sick from my excesses of eating, drinking, and working that I put myself on a vegetarian diet and fresh-air regimen."[4]

Yet without question, Rivera worked more than he played during his time in Spain. On his report card, Chicharro gave him high grades: "He has, from the time he arrived to the present, done numerous landscape works . . . has made much progress, which I do not hesitate to qualify as astonishing. And therefore I am pleased to state that Señor Rivera, my pupil, shows that he has magnificent qualities for the art in which he is engaged."[5]

Traveling through Europe

In the spring of 1909, Rivera took a train headed north to France. He had two years left on his scholarship and he wanted to see more of Europe. To Rivera and many other artists at this time, France meant only one city—Paris.

Rivera arrived in Paris and checked into the Hotel Suez on the main boulevard of what was called the Latin Quarter. This area was a center for artists and writers, and Rivera's room overlooked the bustling street. As in Spain, however, he applied himself as a student, doing little but paint, visit museums, and attend lectures on various topics in art.[6]

Leaving Mexico for Europe

Rivera took a room in a hotel in Madrid, where a friend from San Carlos was already living. The hotel was just a few blocks from El Prado, one of the finest art museums in the world. Rivera would spend a lot of his time there while in Spain, studying the work of great Spanish painters like Goya, El Greco, and Velázquez.

But in the first hours of his arrival in the Spanish capital, Rivera was more anxious to begin his own work. "I was a dynamo of energy," he reported later. "As soon as I located Chicharro's studio, I set up my easel and started to paint. For days on end, I painted from early dawn till past midnight."[3]

Eduardo Chicharro, the teacher with whom Dr. Atl had arranged for Rivera to study, was known for his full-colored portraits. He was a popular figure in the cafés in Madrid, and he introduced Rivera to many artists and writers. One of these was a painter named María Gutiérrez Blanchard. She was also a pupil of Chicharro's, and she and Rivera became fast friends. Blanchard was only four feet tall, with a hunchback resulting from a childhood accident. Walking together through the streets of the city, the tiny Blanchard and the oversized Rivera made a remarkable pair.

Chicharro believed in the importance of getting his students out of the studio to observe the world. The study group traveled extensively throughout the country, often painting street scenes and other landscapes on location.

For two years Rivera studied art in Spain. He painted for long hours and sent many canvases back to Mexico to

Beloff of his love. In the best French he could muster, he declared himself to the woman he saw as a "kind, sensitive, almost unbelievably decent person."[9] Beloff needed time to think about her feelings. She said later, "Diego courted me so fervently that I felt under too much pressure. . . . So I decided to return to Paris, to reflect in peace."[10]

By the fall, Rivera and Beloff were a couple. Rivera continued to work diligently on his artwork. In Paris at that time, large exhibitions called *salons* showed work by artists who were considered noteworthy. A jury made up of important people in the art world—gallery owners, dealers, and museum curators—determined who would make the cut. Rivera's work was selected by the famous Salon des Indépendants of 1910. This was a great honor for Rivera and because of it, his grant money was extended for two more years.[11]

A Triumphant Return to Mexico

Rivera had by now been away from Mexico for four years. He was homesick and wrote the government official in charge of his scholarship to ask if he might return for a visit. His request was granted. Beloff decided that she would go to visit relatives in Russia at the same time. Rivera had been reluctant to commit to marriage, and Beloff believed a year apart would be good for them. "If, after that, he still loved me," she said, "he would return to Paris and we would marry."[12]

Rivera was back on Mexican soil in October 1910. He was met at the railway station by his family and hordes of journalists. In the eyes of the press and the Porfirian government, Rivera had come home to take part in a national celebration. Gala events were planned to mark both the hundredth anniversary of the revolution that freed Mexico from Spain, and the thirty years of rule by Díaz.

Extravagant parties, parades, and bullfights were to be held, presided over by the eighty-year-old dictator. Rivera was to show his work in an art exhibition opening on November 20 at the galleries of his old school, the San Carlos Academy.

It was not Díaz himself but his much younger wife, Doña Carmen Romero Rubio de Díaz, who came to the art show as a representative of the government. She bought a painting Rivera had done in Spain depicting a fisherman and his wife. Doña Carmen's presence at the show, as well as her purchase of his work, signified President Díaz's approval of Rivera.

Revolution!

More than half the paintings in the exhibition sold, and for the first time in his life, Rivera earned a considerable sum of money as an artist. But while he was enjoying his success, in the north of Mexico revolution against the Díaz regime had been proclaimed. The cries of *¡Viva la Revolución!* would soon be heard throughout the country. Only six months later, Porfirio Díaz and his wife would be on a ship sailing to exile in France.

What would come to be known as the Mexican Revolution had begun on the opening day of Rivera's

Leaving Mexico for Europe

> ### Porfiriato
> Through crafty political tactics and simple brute force, Porfirio Díaz ruled Mexico for more than thirty years. Díaz's supporters were members of the ruling class who called themselves Positivistic Scientists. These cientificos claimed that the lands owned by the Indian villages must be taken over in the name of progress. By the end of 1910, to millions of desperately poor Mexicans, Porfirio Díaz had come to stand for all that was wrong with Mexico. The seeds were planted for a revolution.

first one-man show. This complicated and bloody civil war would not end for more than ten years. It would take the lives of more than one million ordinary Mexicans as well as almost all of its greatest heroes.

Rivera did not consider joining the revolutionaries. Instead, he worried about how much longer his government-sponsored scholarship would last, now that the existence of the government itself seemed in question.[13] His immediate action after his art exhibit closed two weeks later was to take a trip into the countryside. He simply wanted to paint some landscapes before returning to France.

Rivera lacked the physical constitution of a soldier. What's more, he was at the cusp of a new career, his pockets flush with the first real cash he had ever earned. At twenty-five, Rivera was more concerned with making art than war.

Diego Rivera: Mexican Muralist

Mexico was undergoing an important revolution, led by hero to the peasants Emiliano Zapata.

Leaving Mexico for Europe

He also claimed he wanted to be with Angelina Beloff. His letters to her from this period reveal intense emotions: "I have spent whole days out in the countryside and little by little have felt closer to your Soul. I have felt the need of you all the time."[14]

Rivera set sail for Europe in the late spring of 1911. Yet despite his letters and telegrams to Beloff alleging that he could not wait to be with her again, he did not go directly to Paris. Instead, Rivera went first to Madrid to visit with some old friends and see an art show.

By the time Rivera arrived in Paris a few weeks later, Beloff was, in her words, "dying of anxiety and sadness."[15] But all was well for the young couple. "Our reunion was rapturous," Rivera said. "Both of us had agreed to wait until this moment to see whether our love was strong enough to withstand the test of separation. We now decided to live together."[16]

Rivera and Beloff did not ever legally marry but considered their relationship to be the same as husband and wife. They spent their first summer back together vacationing in a small village in the mountains of Spain. In the fall they returned to Paris, to an apartment near the subway station in a neighborhood called Montparnasse.

Diego Rivera: Mexican Muralist

Rivera painted this oil on canvas, entitled *Jacques Lipchitz (Portrait of a Young Man)* in 1914, during his cubist period.

Chapter 4

Embracing Cubism

Montparnasse was located on the far edge of Paris's limits, and it seemed a world away from the city. It looked more like the country than an urban center, and it felt different, less formal than the older, more established parts of the city.

Artists were drawn to the neighborhood because of its green rural beauty and because of its cheap rents. Many of the artists' studios were former barns, some of which still had the farm animals living in them. It was not at all unusual to see cows, pigs, or chickens poking around the streets.

But the fact that Montparnasse was a place with few rules had perhaps the greatest appeal for its inhabitants. A free spirit pervaded this artists' colony. What might be considered nontraditional in other sections of Paris was embraced here.

In Montparnasse, café life ruled: The artists spent a good part of every day at the Café Rotonde or the

Café Dome, eating omelets, soups, and fresh bread, drinking coffee and wine, and gossiping or playing chess with friends. At the cafés, Rivera practiced his French, recounting long tales of his life, only some of which were true. Rivera was a great storyteller with a famously wild imagination.

Rivera and Beloff moved into an apartment at 52 Avenue du Maine. Their neighbors included well-known poets, critics, and writers, as well as some of the world's finest painters. Many of these artists were not originally from France but had come to Paris because they believed that the city was the center of the art world. The Spaniard Juan Gris, the Russian Marc Chagall, the Dutch painter Piet Mondrian, and the Italian Amedeo Modigliani all lived within the same few blocks near Rivera.

Rivera and Picasso

In the years just before and after World War I, Pablo Picasso and his friend and colleague Georges Braque began experimenting with a new form of abstract art called cubism. The painters rejected what artists had previously considered hard-and-fast rules of perspective and light. In their place, they painted images that they broke down into many smaller planes, or cubes. The distorted shape of the traditional image would cause the viewer to interpret the art in a new way.

Pablo Picasso

The great artist Pablo Picasso lived nearby as well. At this time Picasso was experimenting with a new style of painting called cubism. In cubist art, the subject often appears to be broken into many shapes and seen from many angles at once. Cubist images are abstract and not always easy to interpret. While today Picasso is considered by many to be the greatest artist of the twentieth century, in 1913 his art was still very controversial, admired by some and strongly disliked by others.

Diego Rivera was one of Picasso's many admirers. But at the beginning of his time in Paris, Rivera was forced to admire him from afar. While he knew that Picasso was one of his close neighbors, Rivera did not yet think himself worthy of an introduction to the great master.[1] Yet he was excited by cubism and began to paint himself in this unconventional style. He would later recall, "I worked hard at my cubist paintings…because everything about the movement fascinated and intrigued me. It was a revolutionary movement, questioning everything that had previously been said and done in art."[2]

Rivera and Beloff soon moved from their apartment to another one around the corner at 26 Rue du Départ. This would be their home for the next seven years. Their studio was on the top floor and had lots of windows with good light for painting. The apartment building was next to the train station. The smoke and noise from the steam locomotives was intense. Most people would have preferred not to be so close to the trains, but Rivera had always been fascinated by them and loved his new location.[3]

Rivera did not consider a visit home during these years. The war in Mexico was at its worst, and with the government upheaval Rivera finally lost his scholarship money. With this serious loss of income, the pressure was on Rivera to produce and sell more of his paintings.

One morning, while Rivera was hard at work in the studio, a friend came knocking at the door with a message: "Picasso sent me to tell you that if you don't go to see him, he's coming to see you."[4] This was a thrilling moment for Rivera and signified his rising status in the art world: The master wanted to meet the young artist.

That same night, the two men had dinner and Picasso critiqued Rivera's paintings. "With this meeting," Rivera reported, "Picasso and I became great friends."[5] This friendship was very important to Rivera. Since Picasso was a Spaniard, the two spoke in Spanish, a joy for Rivera, who found that any other language was still a chore. They both relished the simple pleasures of good food, drink, practical jokes, and passionate conversation. Rivera wrote later, "In Paris, Picasso and I used to have the best times, especially when we were by ourselves. Then we would say things about other painters which we would never tell anybody else."[6]

Another important result of Rivera's friendship with Picasso was the recognition it gave him among other artists. Before Picasso acknowledged Rivera's work, Rivera was known more for his storytelling at the Café

Rotonde than his paintings. After he became friends with Picasso, Rivera's paintings received much more respect.

World War I Erupts

In the summer of 1914, war broke out throughout much of Europe. While some of his colleagues left Paris to report as soldiers in their home armies, Rivera took Angelina Beloff on vacation to Majorca, an island off the Mediterranean coast of Spain. It was peaceful there because Spain did not take sides in the war. The couple stayed three months on what Rivera described as "the wonderful, isolated island, feeling as remote from the conflict on the continent as if we were in the South Seas."[7] Like many others at the time, Rivera believed the war would be over by Christmas; in fact this was a great miscalculation. World War I would not end for another four years.

Rivera and Beloff were safe and relaxed, but they were also broke. Under normal circumstances, Rivera would have sold some of his paintings. The war now made that impossible. In a fortunate turn of events, Beloff was hired to paint the Russian imperial coat-of-arms on the Russian embassy in Barcelona, Spain.

In Barcelona, Rivera got a surprise visit from his mother and sister. They had been worried that he would join the French army and be killed. Though he had not seen his family for more than three years, Rivera was not pleased to see them now. He had never felt any great love for his mother, and he was selfish with his time.

Determined to be rid of his mother as quickly as possible, Rivera borrowed money from the Mexican consulate in Spain to buy tickets on the next ship sailing to Mexico. Being sent away by her son was an embarrassment and disappointment for María del Pilar.[8]

Rivera and Beloff spent the winter in Madrid and in March 1915 returned to their apartment in Paris. With the war raging, there were no buyers for art. Still, the French government provided some assistance in the way of money and food, and the artists of Montparnasse continued life much as before. One painter later recalled,

> we hung about in the Rotonde from morning to night. What else could we do? Where else could we go? . . . Most of us were chronically short of coal and gas and had long since fed to the stove all that could be burnt; the water in our studios was frozen. After a night shivering under thin blankets we would rise late and rush to the café. . . . We would crowd at the door of the toilet to wash. Then we would warm ourselves with hot coffee and croissants.[9]

Zapatista Landscape

Rivera also continued to paint. He had a strong work ethic and felt the need to keep painting even without a potential market for his art. He did what most art critics consider his greatest cubist painting not long after his return to Paris. He called the painting *Zapatista Landscape*. Later he would describe it as "probably the most faithful expression of the Mexican mood that I have ever achieved."[10]

Embracing Cubism

Zapatista Landscape (1915) is considered by many to be Rivera's cubist masterpiece.

By "Mexican mood," Rivera meant a feeling of protest and revolution. The central images of the painting include a rifle and ammunition belt, alongside a Mexican hat and blanket. Emiliano Zapata was a famous revolutionary hero, whose followers were called Zapatistas. In *Zapatista Landscape,* for the first time in his art, Rivera demonstrated his support for the revolutionaries in his homeland.

The painting was good enough to attract the interest of a well-connected art dealer named Léonce Rosenberg. He represented the best cubist painters, including Picasso. Rosenberg agreed to pay Rivera a monthly salary in exchange for the right to sell the cubist paintings Rivera would create.

Rosenberg introduced Rivera to the business part of the art world. Before, Rivera had painted whatever he was in the mood to do. Under contract to a dealer, he was expected to paint at least four canvases a month. He would be paid more for a portrait than a landscape. Likewise, a larger painting would bring more than a smaller one.[11] While the arrangement with Rosenberg might have squelched Rivera's creativity a bit, it assured him and Beloff a steadier income.

Now that they could afford it, the couple decided to start a family. A son they named Diego, and called Dieguito, was born in August 1916. Though Rivera was pleased to be a father, he expected Beloff to take full care of the infant. He was not willing to allow any distractions from his painting.

Abandoning Cubism

By this time Rivera had become internationally recognized as a cubist painter. His work was shown at an exhibition in New York City. At this show, Rivera's canvases hung alongside those of Picasso, Van Gogh, and Cézanne. His work sold well and his dealer was happy.

Yet Rivera was not satisfied. He believed that cubism was just one way of painting and that, after more than four years, he had learned all he could from it. He wanted to experiment with alternative methods. Unfortunately, Rosenberg refused to represent Rivera unless he painted in the cubist style. When Rivera turned away from the technique, Rosenberg dropped him as a client.

With the loss of their monthly income, life became extremely difficult for Rivera and Beloff. The war continued to devastate Europe, making food and supplies scarce. The couple could not afford to buy fuel to heat their apartment. The bitter cold was too much for their son, who had been malnourished and sickly for some time. At only fourteen months old, Dieguito developed pneumonia and died.

Dieguito's death was a crushing blow for his parents. Rivera tried to divert his grief through work. In the months following, he did more than twenty-five paintings in both oil and watercolor. These paintings contained elements of cubism but were less abstract.

Years later Rivera would claim to be able to pinpoint the exact moment when he knew he was done with cubism and had found a new course in his painting:

Diego Rivera: Mexican Muralist

Soon after painting *The Architect*, Rivera abandoned cubism. The artist wanted to explore different painting styles.

Embracing Cubism

I started on the new path one beautifully light afternoon in 1917. . . . I saw a curbside pushcart filled with peaches. Suddenly, my whole being was filled with this commonplace object. I stood there transfixed, my eyes absorbing every detail. With unbelievable force, the texture, forms, and colors of the peaches seemed to reach out to me. I rushed back to my studio and began my experiments that very day.[12]

Unfortunately for Angelina Beloff, work could not provide the distraction it did for Rivera. She continued to mourn for baby Dieguito, and Rivera did little to comfort her. Instead, for many reasons, it began to look very much like their relationship was about to end.

Diego Rivera: Mexican Muralist

Rivera touches up a portrait of Mexican dictator Porfirio Díaz, part of his mural.

Chapter 5
Rivera's First Murals

An artist who lived life to the fullest, Rivera often acted impulsively, without first considering others. This was true of his relationship with women. It was no secret that for about a year, Diego Rivera had been involved with another woman, Russian artist Marevna Vorobev. Marevna had a very different temperament from Rivera's practical and patient wife, Angelina. Marevna Vorobev was quick-tempered and impulsive.

Rivera's love affair with Vorobev was obviously difficult for Angelina Beloff. Things became even more complicated when Rivera fathered a daughter, Marika, with his lover. Rivera ended his affair with Vorobev, but his relationship with Beloff was never the same. Rivera would acknowledge much later that Beloff was a good-hearted, honest person who "received from me all the heartache and misery that a man can inflict upon a woman."[1]

The Italian Renaissance Influence

In November 1918, World War I finally came to an end. More than 8 million soldiers had been killed, with another 23 million wounded. Many men who came home from the front were permanently affected by poisonous mustard gas, a chemical weapon that damaged their nervous systems. Rivera learned details of these horrors from an army surgeon named Elie Fauré.

Fauré was a doctor, but he was also a well-known art historian. Rivera painted a portrait of Fauré in his uniform, and the two became good friends. Fauré was a scholar who had researched and written many books about Italian Renaissance painters. He encouraged Rivera to go to Italy to see in person the artwork of the fifteenth-century masters.

Rivera took Fauré's advice and traveled throughout Italy, sketching hundreds of drawings. Angelina Beloff remained in Paris, aware that her life with Rivera was coming to a close.

In Italy, Rivera studied mosaics, sculpture, and paintings. But it was the frescoes by artists like Giotto di Bondone, Piero della Francesa, and Raphael Sanzio that interested him the most. These paintings on plaster walls, with their intense coloring, appealed to him in a special way. In Italy, Rivera began to think of his own art in a new light. He also began to think about going back to Mexico.

In May 1921, Elie Fauré reported, "Rivera has returned from Italy, loaded with drawings, loaded with new sensations, loaded with ideas, boiling over with new myths, thin (yes!) and radiant. He says that he will soon be leaving for Mexico, but I don't believe a word of it."[2]

Yet Rivera would prove Fauré wrong. In a short time, he packed up his few belongings and prepared to return to his homeland. He promised Angelina Beloff that he would send for her as soon as he could. In fact they would never see each other again.

Return to a Changed Mexico

The ten years Rivera had spent in Europe were some of the most destructive and chaotic years in Mexican history. Rivera returned home to a very different country from the one he had left. Porfirio Díaz was dead, and the civil war was over. Mexico had a new constitution and a new president, a war hero named Alvaro Obregón.

Obregón's primary task was to begin the rebuilding of his war-torn country. One of his first acts as president was to name the renowned Mexican philosopher José Vasconcelos as minister of education. Only thirty-eight years old, Vasconcelos was by all accounts a brilliant and resourceful man. His stated goal was to end illiteracy in Mexico. With a vast budget provided by the new government, he had new schools and libraries constructed. Most significantly for Rivera, Vasconcelos had ambitious plans to fund new forays in Mexican art and culture.

Rivera had come home at the right time. Immediately upon his arrival, he went to show his work to Vasconcelos, who offered him a university teaching job. Rivera accepted the post, particularly when he learned that his parents were ill and in need of his support.

But Rivera had his sights set on another role in Vasconcelos's ministry. Vasconcelos had announced his intention to commission artists to paint murals on public buildings throughout Mexico. This was the job Rivera wanted.

Rivera was elated to be home again. He said afterward:

> "My homecoming produced an esthetic exhilaration which is impossible to describe. It was as if I were being born anew, born into a new world. All the colors I saw appeared to be heightened; they were clearer, richer, finer, and more full of light. The dark tones had a depth they never had in Europe."[3]

In November, Vasconcelos invited Rivera and several other painters to accompany him to a remote part of southeastern Mexico called the Yucatán Peninsula. Here for the first time Diego Rivera saw the ruins of classic Mayan civilization. The Maya were a highly sophisticated pre-Hispanic people of Mexico. They had a thorough understanding of mathematics and astronomy and they made the world's first accurate calendar.

In the Yucatán Peninsula, Rivera studied the pyramid-shaped Mayan temples. He made many sketches of the ruins and paid close attention to the murals that decorated the buildings. Before this visit, Rivera had had little exposure to the art of his Mexican forebears. This trip would produce for him a lifelong interest in early Mexican art.

Not long after Rivera's return from the Yucatán Peninsula, his father died. Despite the extended period in Europe during which Rivera had almost no contact with his father, Diego was deeply saddened.[4] Rivera remembered a father who "dedicated his life to freedom and progress" and who took great pride in his son's artistic achievements.[5]

Guadalupe Marín

After his father's burial, Rivera got the job he had been waiting for: Vasconcelos asked him to paint a mural on the walls of the auditorium of the National Preparatory School.

The importance of making art available in a public space so that it could be enjoyed by anyone who happened to pass by—rich or poor—was an idea first put forth to Rivera by the art scholar Elie Fauré. In his campaign to bring art to every Mexican, this was Vasconcelos's goal as well. Vasconcelos had high standards for this art of the people. "One of the imperatives of our program," he said later, "was to put the public in contact with great artists rather than mediocrities."[6]

The room Rivera had been assigned to paint was used as a lecture and concert hall. It had a stage and a large pipe organ that sat in an alcove beneath a broad archway. Rivera believed that the architecture of the space should

Diego Rivera: Mexican Muralist

Painting large-scale murals required Rivera to work on moveable platforms high above the floor.

Rivera's First Murals

be incorporated into the painting itself. The archway served as the center of his mural.

Rivera chose as his theme the creation of the world. It would take him more than a year to finish the painting. It was the first time he had attempted a mural, so he had to learn how to paint using a scaffold—a movable platform that permitted him to reach the high parts of the wall. Another reason the mural took such a long time was that Rivera chose to paint it with a technique called encaustic. Encaustic is a complicated method that includes melting wax along with the paint.

For the female figures in the mural, Rivera hired a model named Guadalupe Marín. Rivera described her as "a strange and marvelous-looking creature, nearly six feet tall. ... Her face was an Indian's, the mouth with its full powerful lips open, the corners drooping like those of a tiger."[7] Before he completed the mural, Rivera had fallen in love with Guadalupe Marín.

Diego and Lupe, as he called her, were married in a church in her hometown of Guadalajara, in June 1922. They moved to a house in the center of Mexico City near the busy fruit and flower markets. Two daughters, Guadalupe (nicknamed Pico) and Ruth, were born in the next few years. Lupe Marín was known as a great cook and hostess, and their home became the meeting place for their artist friends.

Los Tres Grandes

Rivera had recently joined the Communist Party, and many of the gatherings in his home focused on politics.

Communists believe in a system of government in which nothing is owned privately; instead, everything is owned by the state, and wealth is to be shared by all citizens. Rivera and his fellow Communists viewed it as their mission to make art that would remain on permanent display for the people of Mexico to share equally.

For these artists, murals were the preferred art form because they were painted on buildings where they could readily be seen by the public. Unlike easel paintings, murals could not be bought and sold. The muralists even chose to think of themselves as being more like housepainters than elite artists. They formed a trade union, as plumbers or electricians do, to protect their economic interests even though they were not making much money. Rivera earned about $2 a day painting the National Preparatory School.[8]

Among Rivera's colleagues, two others stood out for their talent and strong political leanings. One was David Alfaro Siqueiros. Ten years younger than Rivera, Siqueiros had fought in the Mexican Revolution and believed fervently in the Communist cause. The other artist was José Clemente Orozco, whose work often depicted tragic images related to the Revolution. Together, Rivera, Siqueiros, and Orozco would become known internationally as the most prominent of the Mexican muralists, "Los Tres Grandes," or the Big Three.[9]

Mural at the Ministry of Education

While Rivera put the finishing touches on his first mural, Vasconcelos was already waiting with a new commission.

Communism

In 1848, the German philosophers Karl Marx and Friedrich Engels wrote *The Communist Manifesto*, one of the most influential political writings in history. Marx and Engels sympathized with workers. They viewed workers as being in a constant struggle against the powers of business and government. The central idea of Communism is that all people should be equal in wealth and social status. In 1917, a revolution in Russia overthrew the government there and set up the first Communist state.

This was a much larger job, and it was a project very close to Vasconcelos's heart. He wanted Rivera to paint the Ministry of Education building.

The building was brand-new, though it had been modeled on a centuries-old convent. It was made of stone and stucco, and stood three stories high and two city blocks long. It had a vast, rectangular interior courtyard, with open patios. Each of the offices in the building stood beneath a vaulted archway. There are 128 walls between these archways. Rivera was to paint a mural on each of these walls.

Rivera knew from the start that encaustic would prove too time-consuming for a project of this size. This time he would have to learn the ancient technique of fresco painting. *Fresco* means "fresh" in Italian. The artist paints on a fresh, damp plaster wall. He has to work

Diego Rivera: Mexican Muralist

This detail of Rivera's fresco in Mexico's Governor's Palace depicts Adolf Hitler as leader of the people. Albert Einstein appears in the lower left corner.

quickly and is in a constant race to make any changes in the paint before the plaster dries.

The first days were rough for Rivera. A friend reported one night seeing Rivera's scaffold "shaking as though an earthquake was about to start. Peering up through the darkness I saw the obscure mass of the painter. He was sobbing uncontrollably, and furiously erasing his entire day's work with a little trowel, like a small boy in a rage flattening his sandcastle."[10]

It was an assistant to Rivera who solved the situation for him. Using a method he remembered seeing his father, a house painter, use to paint stucco walls, Xavier Guerrero devised a technique for fresco. He mixed the juice of over-ripened cactus leaves into the paint. Guerrero's tinkering finally allowed Rivera to work.

And work he did, sometimes as long as eighteen hours a day. During the more than four years it took Rivera to complete the Ministry building, he mastered the technique of fresco painting. He was disciplined and systematic. His assistants would prepare the plaster walls the night before and Rivera would climb the scaffold at dawn to paint. He wrote:

> *When I first arrive, I paint all the outlined figures in gray on the section which has been prepared for that day. At this time, too, I make all last-minute revisions. Then I do the final work in color, using pigments which have been ground for me by my helpers and mixed with distilled water into a paste. At the end of a day's work, I stand back at a fair distance and criticize what I have just done. If, as sometimes happens, I am*

> *dissatisfied, I have the whole area cleaned and a new coat of lime laid on. Then I redo the work the next day.*[11]

As his theme for the frescoes, Rivera chose a celebration of the work and life of the Mexican people. One area focused on industry and agriculture, another on the arts, and a third on festivals and revolutions. José Vasconcelos's goal was to bring culture to the masses, and the pre-Hispanic cultures from Mexico had a long tradition of pictorial narratives. At the Ministry of Education building, Rivera's paintings would communicate culture to the people. With the murals on the Ministry of Education building, Rivera would establish himself as the foremost painter in Mexico.

Chapter 6

DIEGO AND FRIDA

One of the consequences of painting murals in public places was the lack of privacy afforded to Rivera. As he became well known, Mexicans and tourists alike began to visit his work sites to watch him paint. A close friend and biographer of Rivera, Bertram D. Wolfe, described him as "one of the 'sights' of Mexico City."[1]

Wolfe wrote about his own introduction to the artist: "It was on the scaffold here that I first got to know him well: a bulky, genial, slow-moving, frog-faced man, in weather-worn overalls, huge Stetson hat, cartridge belt, large pistol, vast paint-and-plaster-stained shoes."[2]

Rivera carried a pistol as protection for himself and his crew. It is unlikely that they were ever in any real danger, but it was not unusual for men in Mexico at this time to have guns. One artist friend of Rivera's wrote, "I was told that he fired a gun into the air while standing on his scaffold. When asked why he said it was to frighten off hostile journalists."[3]

A Life-Changing Meeting

It was true that Rivera did not like to be interrupted while he was working. One day in 1926, while he was high on the scaffold at the Ministry of Education, a young woman persisted in calling up to him in an effort to get his attention. Made curious by her boldness, Rivera finally set aside his palette and climbed down from his perch.

What he saw close up appealed to him: "Her hair was long; dark and thick eyebrows met above her nose. They seemed like the wings of a blackbird, their black arches framing two extraordinary brown eyes."[4] She introduced herself as Frida Kahlo. She had brought some of her paintings to show Rivera, and she wanted an honest opinion of their worth.

Rivera was by this time a well-known artist. It took courage for Kahlo to approach him. That was her nature. Twenty years old, Kahlo had graduated as one of only thirty-five girls among the two thousand students at the National Preparatory School. She had planned to enter medical school. When a trolley car she was riding crashed, and one of its iron handrails pierced her midsection, Kahlo had to change her plans. Her intensely painful recovery confined her to bed for months in a full body cast. It was during this time that she taught herself to paint.

DIEGO AND FRIDA

Frida Kahlo was a young student when Rivera met her. The two would feed each other artistically for the rest of their lives.

Diego Rivera was impressed by Kahlo's artwork and attracted to her independent spirit. As he later confessed, "I did not know it then, but Frida had already become the most important fact in my life."[5]

Frida Kahlo

Often overshadowed during her lifetime by the more famous Rivera, Frida Kahlo was a great artist in her own right. While Rivera executed his huge public murals, Kahlo pursued work in the opposite direction. Her small, very personal paintings, often done on canvases of tin, glass, or wood, reflected her strong political views. Her honest self-portraits, in which she closely examined subjects such as childbirth and death, are among her most powerful works.

National School of Agriculture Mural

Diego and Lupe's marriage had its difficulties. Rivera recalled, "Lupe was a beautiful, spirited animal but her jealousy and possessiveness gave our life together a wearying, hectic intensity. And I, unfortunately, was not a faithful husband."[6] At one point Lupe became so enraged with her husband that she ground up a valuable stone sculpture he had purchased, mixed it in with some sauce, and served it to him for dinner.

The couple divorced in 1927 while Rivera was working two jobs at once. He had not yet finished with the walls of the Ministry of Education building when he began another mural project in a chapel at the National School of Agriculture. This school was in a town called Chapingo, about an hour outside Mexico City.

The motto of the agriculture school was "Here we teach the exploitation of the earth, not of man," a creed that appealed to the Communist in Rivera. His murals at the chapel applaud nature, the worker, and Communism as the form of government that Rivera thought best served the worker.

Many art historians believe the murals at the Ministry of Education building and those at Chapingo Chapel are among the very best of Rivera's work. Painting at both sites simultaneously, the artist was certainly in a period of high creative energy. Rivera's activity may have caught up to him one day when, for the only time in his career, he fell headfirst from the scaffolding and fractured his skull.[7]

When he was just about finished at the Ministry of Education building, Rivera decided to take a break from work. He planned a trip to Russia while the country was celebrating the tenth anniversary of the 1917 Revolution, which had brought the Communists to power.

Rivera was treated as a celebrity in Russia. He was asked to sit in a special area roped off for important guests, where he was able to view the many parades and other festivities. From this seat, Rivera made a series of about fifty drawings and watercolor paintings, which he would call the "May Day Sketches." He was even introduced to Joseph Stalin, who was to become the Communist Party dictator.

Marrying "The Devil"

When he returned home, Rivera finally painted the last frescoes at the Ministry of Education. These great murals had taken him almost six years to complete. It was now late 1928. A year had passed since Frida Kahlo had interrupted him on the scaffold to ask his opinion of her paintings.

At a party given by a mutual friend, the two artists met for a second time. In a clumsy attempt to impress her, Rivera fired a gun at a record player when he did not like the music that was playing.[8] The bullet hole, or something else, seemed to work. Despite a twenty-year age difference, Rivera and Frida Kahlo were soon married.

They made an unusual-looking pair. Rivera was a foot taller than Kahlo and outweighed her by nearly two hundred pounds. Frida was an unconventional dresser. She liked to wear old-fashioned long Mexican skirts and shawls. When he was not in his painting overalls and smock, Diego favored modern Western suits and cowboy hats.

Before their wedding, Frida's father warned Diego that his daughter could be tough, "a devil" as he put it, but Rivera was not dissuaded.[9] In fact, he very much admired Kahlo's spirit, what he called the "fire in her eyes."[10] Rivera also respected Kahlo's artistic vision. Bertram Wolfe later wrote, "He discussed her painting

Diego and Frida

Although Diego and Frida made an unusual pair, they fell madly in love and married in 1929.

with her, then finding that her taste was swift and sure, began asking for her opinion of his own work. So far as I know, he never consulted any other person, man or woman, in the years of his maturity."[11]

Two Important Commissions

The year 1929 was an important one for Rivera. He married Frida Kahlo and he was hired to paint two very prominent murals. First, the Mexican government commissioned him to paint a history of Mexico on the main stairway of the National Palace. The National Palace is the building where the president works. That he was asked to paint this building indicates Rivera was considered at this time the greatest painter in Mexico.

The second prestigious commission Rivera received was from the United States government. He was asked by the American ambassador to Mexico, Dwight W. Morrow, to paint the Palace of Cortés in the town of Cuernavaca. Hernando de Cortés was the sixteenth-century Spanish conquistador who conquered Mexico. Morrow asked Rivera to paint the history of the region beginning with the Spanish conquest. The mural would then be presented as a gift to Mexico from the United States.

Rivera began work on the National Palace but quickly interrupted it to begin in Cuernavaca. This stop-and-go course of action would be a pattern for him at the National Palace for the next twenty-two years. Rivera later poked fun at himself, writing, "To my friends it has

Diego and Frida

This detail of Rivera's Mexican history mural for the National Palace depicts the arrival of Hernán Cortés in 1519.

become a joke to say, 'Have you heard the news? Diego has finished painting the stairway.'"[12]

The monumental National Palace murals are among the first works of art anywhere to depict Mexican history from the Aztecs through the Mexican Revolution. Many of the scenes are of bloody battles. To Rivera, the history of Mexico was a succession of rebellions by the people against corrupt governments and a greedy Catholic church.[13]

At the Palace of Cortés, Rivera painted themes in a similar vein. In sixteen frescoes he showed the Mexican people taking arms against foreign conquerors and evil Mexican dictators. Here, also, Rivera blasts a church he had viewed since childhood as uncaring.

While the National Palace and Cuernavaca commissions were among the most important Rivera would ever receive, the Communist Party did not approve of them. For doing business with the Mexican and U.S. governments, the party expelled Rivera from its membership in 1929.

Rivera would continue to think of himself as a Communist for the rest of his life. Yet he was too much of a freethinker not to stray from the party's strict doctrine. Examining his expulsion years later, Rivera said that he was punished by the party for refusing to believe every word that it published.[14]

In the midst of all this tumult, Rivera accepted the job of director at his old school, the San Carlos Academy. As director, Rivera was a surprisingly stern taskmaster.

Imitating what he claimed was the school regimen followed by Leonardo da Vinci, Rivera instituted a curriculum in which the students were expected to work all day and take their classes at night, seven days a week.[15] Neither the professors nor the pupils were happy with this new arrangement and made it clear that they wanted Rivera removed from his post.

After the Communist Party expulsion and the problems at San Carlos, Rivera and Kahlo decided they needed a change of scene. Just before Christmas 1930, the couple left for their first trip north of the Río Bravo, known in the United States as the Rio Grande.

DIEGO RIVERA: MEXICAN MURALIST

A detail from Rivera's sprawling mural celebrating industry in Detroit shows Ford Motor Company machinists at work.

Chapter 7

AMERICAN COMMISSIONS

Many Mexicans had a negative perception of the United States. This dated back to the U.S-Mexican war (1846–1848), when the United States gained lands that made up half its territory, including what are now the states of California, Texas, Arizona, New Mexico, Colorado, and Utah. Mexicans who had owned the land that was ceded to the United States suddenly went from profitable ranch owners to men with no property and no prospects. Some moved away from their homes; those who remained were forced to work menial jobs.

By the time of the Great Depression in the 1930s, the economic situation in the United States had gotten worse. With a fourth of the nation unemployed, Caucasian Americans began demanding the jobs held by Latinos, jobs they had previously considered beneath them. Half a million Mexicans were deported, even many who possessed American citizenship.

The Mexican-American War

President James K. Polk was elected in 1844 on a campaign promise to expand U.S. territories in the Southwest. When Texas was made a state in 1845, the United States claimed the right to all lands north of the Rio Grande. War broke out between the United States and Mexico. The Treaty of Guadalupe-Hidalgo in 1848 fixed the border at the Rio Grande, with the United States paying Mexico $15 million for what amounted to half of Mexico's former territory.

San Francisco

Rivera traveled north in 1930 because he had been offered a good job. The year before, the American Institute of Architects had awarded him its Fine Arts Gold Medal. After this, Rivera had received commissions to create two frescoes in San Francisco. The president of the San Francisco Art Commission, William Gerstle, wanted Rivera to paint a wall at the California School of Fine Arts. Gerstle had been given one of Rivera's paintings as a gift and had first thought little of it. Then, he reported, "To my surprise, I could not take my eyes off it, and in the course of a few days . . . I began to feel that what I had taken for a crude daub had more power and beauty than any other of my pictures."[1]

The second mural Rivera was hired to paint was in the restaurant at the newly built San Francisco Stock Exchange. San Francisco had been known for its murals since the city began rebuilding after its near-total destruction in the great earthquake of 1906. In fact, some San Francisco artists had even traveled to Mexico to watch Rivera at work.

When Rivera and Frida Kahlo arrived in San Francisco from Mexico, it was considered such an important event that the famous photographer Ansel Adams was at the train station to take their picture. The *San Francisco Chronicle* gave its readers a colorful description of Rivera, "beaming behind an ever-present cigar, his clothes bulkier than his big frame, a broad-brimmed hat of distinct rural type on his curly locks."[2]

Of the two murals Rivera had been hired to paint, the one at the stock exchange was a departure for him. The fresco was to be done on the wall of a stairway leading to a private eating club. All of Rivera's previous works had been done on the exterior walls of buildings that were open to the public. The fact that a Communist was going to paint the walls of a stock exchange, an institution most closely tied to capitalism, was a remarkable thing in itself.

From the first, Rivera was happy in the United States. San Francisco socialites gave many fancy parties in his honor."[3] It was at one of these parties that Rivera was introduced to the tennis star Helen Wills Moody.

Moody was an athletic beauty whom Rivera decided would make the perfect model to represent California in his painting. The two became fast friends, Moody driving up and down the steep streets of the city in her two-seater Cadillac, with the oversized Rivera crushed in beside her.[4]

Rivera called the stock exchange mural *Allegory of California*. As Mother California, Helen Wills Moody's face and upper torso loom over images of the natural resources for which the state is known: gold, fruits, vegetables, and petroleum. Farm and industrial workers surround her, proud expressions on their faces. A young boy plays with a model airplane, symbolizing the future.[5]

The mural reflects Rivera's enormous pleasure at being in California and his approval of its booming industry. The effects of the Depression had not yet made their mark on the state. Ever since he was a little boy, Rivera had been fascinated by the way machines worked. In industrial America, he was able to include these machines in his paintings.

The California School of Fine Arts mural was entitled *The Making of a Fresco*. It took Rivera only five weeks to complete. It is a picture of Rivera himself, with his back to the viewer, supervising his assistants on the scaffold. Like the other San Francisco mural, this one includes images of industry—steel, skyscrapers, airplanes—and is optimistic in tone.

When he finished this second mural at the end of May 1931, Rivera and Kahlo returned to Mexico, where he continued his work on the National Palace frescoes. He had asked two of his assistants to do some painting in his absence, but was not happy with the results. "They had imitated my style," he reported, "yet their work looked

American Commissions

Rivera soon became a sought-after painter. He was commissioned to create murals in many public and private spaces in the United States and Mexico.

so different to me from what I did with my own hands, that I could not let it stand. I was obliged to scratch out every stroke of their painting."[6]

New York City

While on the scaffold in the midst of reworking the mural, Rivera was visited by a representative from the Museum of Modern Art in New York City. She had come to Mexico to offer him a one-man show at the museum. Rivera was thrilled. "To every modern artist," he explained later, "this is the pinnacle of professional success."[7]

Rivera and Kahlo sailed to New York on a ship called the *Morro Castle*. By 1931, New York City, unlike San Francisco, had been hit hard by the Great Depression. Rivera saw thousands of men out of work and families waiting in long lines for food handouts. Rivera had seen poverty in Mexico City and in London, but not on the scale he witnessed in New York City.

His museum show was to include about 150 drawings, oil paintings, and watercolors. Since he could not, of course, remove his murals from the walls where they were painted, Rivera duplicated scenes from some of them on portable panels. These frames weighed more than a thousand pounds each. Rivera also painted a new fresco based on his impressions of New York City. The work was entitled *Frozen Assets*. It depicted a dismal city of skyscrapers and subway cars, angry police, and unemployed, homeless people.

American Commissions

Rivera's show at the Museum of Modern Art was an enormous success. The newspaper reviews were glowing, and the public came out in droves. More people came to see Rivera's artwork than had come to see the museum's previous one-man show devoted to the famous French painter Henri Matisse.[8]

Before the exhibition at the Museum of Modern Art, Rivera had been well known primarily in Mexico. After the New York show, his name was known to the world. Some of the wealthiest and most influential people in the United States now wanted to buy his art.

On to Detroit

From New York City, Rivera and Kahlo went by train to Detroit, Michigan. Edsel Ford, the son of Henry Ford, wanted Rivera to paint a series of murals at the Detroit Institute of Arts. Ford offered to pay $15,000 for the work at the museum, a large amount of money in 1932, particularly in a time of economic depression.

Rivera was very excited by his subject matter. The automobiles and the mass production assembly lines used to manufacture them fascinated him. He spent his first month at the Ford plant in Dearborn, Michigan, making hundreds of sketches of both the machinery in the plants and the men who worked there. He told an American friend, "Your engineers are your great artists."[9]

To Rivera, the machine meant freedom for the worker. The twenty-seven frescoes at the Detroit museum were meant to reflect this faith in technology and the men who used it. Rivera worked very long hours, often beginning

Diego Rivera: Mexican Muralist

Rivera enjoyed his time in the United States, but Kahlo struggled with the cultural differences.

his sketching on the scaffold at midnight so he would be ready to paint at dawn.[10]

Sometimes Rivera was filmed by a cameraman. Edsel Ford was fascinated by the process Rivera used at work but was too busy with his own job to take the time to observe him. Instead, he simply had the artist filmed and watched the movie clips at night.

For Frida Kahlo, this was a difficult time. She became pregnant but then had a miscarriage. Then she got word from Mexico that her mother was dying. Kahlo went home immediately to Mexico City, leaving Rivera to fend for himself. He continued working anywhere from eight to sixteen hours a day, with few breaks.

Rivera did not even stop to eat. He had decided to go on a drastic diet. For a month, this three-hundred-pound giant of a man ate nothing every day but four lemons, two grapefruits, six oranges, and a salad.[11] He lost more than one hundred pounds and had to borrow clothes from one of his assistants. When Kahlo returned from Mexico, she did not recognize her husband.[12]

In March 1933, the murals at the Detroit Institute of Arts opened to the public. Nearly one hundred thousand people came to see them in the first month alone. Rivera was pleased with the results of his efforts, but not everyone approved of the murals. A Catholic priest in the United States who had a radio talk show criticized Rivera for what he viewed as anti-Church messages painted in the frescoes.

Diego Rivera: Mexican Muralist

At this same time in other parts of the world, far more vicious attacks were being made on others. In Germany, Adolf Hitler had just taken power. Already his stormtroopers were arresting and killing innocent people there. In Italy, the dictator Benito Mussolini was crushing everyone who disagreed with his government. His suspicions went beyond politics. To Mussolini, anyone who liked modern art was dangerous.

Like Diego Rivera, Mexican muralists David Alfaro Siqueiros and José Clemente Orozco also chose to paint in the United States in the 1930s. Siqueiros did most of his work in southern California, while Orozco worked there and also painted a multipaneled mural at Dartmouth

Rivera works on his mural at Rockefeller Center. This triumph would eventually be destroyed, much to the artist's dismay.

College in New Hampshire. Though Siqueiros and Orozco would achieve great fame as Mexican muralists, it was always Rivera whose reputation was most prominent.

After Detroit, Rivera and Kahlo went to New York City, where they were about to go head-to-head with the Rockefellers. Although the trip would end disastrously with the destruction of Rivera's mural, up until that point Rivera very much enjoyed his time in Manhattan's restaurants, museums, and theaters. Kahlo, on the other hand, wanted only to return to her native Mexico. After nearly four years, she was tired of being in America, the country she called "Gringolandia."[13]

Just before Christmas 1933, Rivera and Kahlo sailed home. Their time in the United States had been a roller coaster of sorts. What they wanted now was some quiet time. Little did they know, things were not going to be any more tranquil in Mexico.

Diego Rivera: Mexican Muralist

Rivera returned to Mexico in bad shape, both physically and emotionally.

Chapter 8

A Return to Mexico

Back in Mexico, Rivera's health was suffering. The drastic weight loss he had experienced in Detroit was taking a toll on his body. The shock to his system was so great that Rivera's doctor prescribed a different kind of diet: he must eat like the three-hundred-pound man he usually was, in order to be "reinflated and not disinflated again under any circumstances."[1]

But more significantly, Rivera was unhappy. The wrecking of his mural by the Rockefellers had taken a huge toll on him. In San Francisco and Detroit, he had felt at the height of his artistic powers.[2] When the mural came crashing down in New York City, Rivera came crashing down with it.

To distract himself from his depression, Rivera went to work. At the request of a friend who was building a fancy hotel in Mexico City called the Hotel Reforma, he painted a four-paneled mural in the dining room. He chose as the mural's theme Mexican folk festivals. Among the merry scenes, Rivera added political cartoons that were not appropriate for a hotel. One cartoon mocked a government official. He also made fun of tourists in Mexico.

The hotel owner paid Rivera for his work but then had his brother paint over some of the offending scenes. Rivera went to court to keep the hotelier from further damaging the artwork. The judge ruled in Rivera's favor and fined the hotel owner for forgery.

Still, Rivera could not force the proprietor to display his mural. Instead, it was hidden away. Rivera would not paint another mural for six years. After the fiasco at the RCA Building and now this rebuff, he turned his back on what had brought him his greatest fame.

Turning to Portraiture

In place of the wall, Rivera went to the easel. Wealthy men and women had been asking him to paint their portraits for a long time. For Rivera, portrait painting was easy money and required less effort than mural painting. He did not have to employ assistants, as he did on the murals. Also, his political views did not come into question. Most important, he did not have to worry that when he had finished the piece it would be covered up or demolished.

Rivera painted the high society of Mexico City—rich businessmen, movie stars, doctors, musicians, and nightclub owners. Not all of his subjects were Mexican-born. At this time, Mexico City was a hotbed of cultural activity, drawing a mix of people from all over the world. Sophisticated patrons from the United States and Europe all wanted to be painted by the famous Rivera.

Rivera painted those close to him as well. He did a portrait of his former wife, Lupe Marín, with whom he remained good friends. He painted a series of pictures of Frida Kahlo, and he produced another series of self-portraits. In these, he never shied from a truthful image, even when it was unflattering. As one critic wrote, "It is Rivera as he knows himself, and he knows himself well."[3]

Finally, Rivera painted the faces of many who were neither famous nor related to him. Rivera turned his focus on the indigenous people of Mexico. Indian men, women, and children began to dominate his easel paintings as much as they had always been integral to his murals. Often the men are shown hard at work, carrying shovels and axes. Rivera painted Indian women selling flowers from baskets tied high on their backs, or sitting on the ground folding tortillas.

Rivera was interested in depicting the simple beauty of the Indians' everyday existence. He was moved with equal passion to make a political statement against those whom he viewed as their oppressors: foreigners and wealthy Mexicans. Frida Kahlo would later write, "He has only one great social concern: to raise the standard of living of the Mexican Indians, whom he loves so deeply."[4]

Rivera worked both in oil and in watercolor. He produced hundreds of easel paintings. It was an extremely

Diego Rivera: Mexican Muralist

Rivera eventually returned to murals. Here, he sketches out a mural depicting Pan-American unity.

had been painted blue because of the Mexican belief that the color blue could ward off evil spirits.

Since Stalin had vowed to have Trotsky killed, the *Casa Azul* was immediately placed under heavy guard. Police with rifles were stationed outside the house and on the roof. Rivera even bought the house next door as an extra precaution.[5]

At first, all seemed to go well. The Trotskys were engaging intellectuals, and Rivera and Kahlo enjoyed their company. Then Leon Trotsky began an affair with Frida Kahlo. For her part, Kahlo may have been less interested in Trotsky than in getting back at her husband for his many infidelities over the years, including a tryst with her sister, Cristina.[6]

In any event, the affair soon ended and Kahlo left for New York City. She had been offered a one-woman exhibition at a gallery there. Wanting to show her independence from Rivera, who had always preferred her long braids and traditional dress, Kahlo cut her hair very short and exchanged her Mexican-inspired clothing for New York designer clothes.[7]

Six months later, Kahlo returned to learn that Rivera wanted a divorce. She would continue to live in her side of the house with the bridge. After the separation from Rivera, she created what many critics considered some of her finest paintings. As for Leon Trotsky, his stay in Mexico ended in August 1940, after Stalin's assassins finally caught up with him at his home.

prolific period for him and a time when his interest in Mexican customs and folklore was greatest.

Many of the same wealthy patrons who posed for his portraits now bought Rivera's paintings of Mexican Indians to hang on their walls. A Rivera painting was an expensive painting. None of the native Mexicans who figured so largely in his work could afford to own one themselves.

Sheltering Trotsky

Rivera's marriage to Frida Kahlo had always been complicated. At this time, the two decided to create a living arrangement with a twist. The artists built studios next door to each other connected by a bridge. Both understood that while they loved each other deeply, their relationship always would be a stormy one. Separate but connected homes seemed like a good compromise.

In early 1937, Rivera was drawn into a political situation that put him at great risk. The Communist Party ruling Russia had split into two factions, one headed by the dictator Joseph Stalin, and the other by Leon Trotsky, an exiled former Russian leader. Trotsky had been sentenced to death by Stalin. Trotsky and his wife, Natalia, had been hiding in Norway. They now needed a new place to stay.

Rivera persuaded the Mexican government to offer political asylum to the Trotskys. He then invited them to live as guests in Frida Kahlo's childhood home, a dwelling called the *Casa Azul,* or Blue House. The home

A Return to Mexico

Frida Kahlo suffered through many of Rivera's infidelities during their time together.

Remarriage

After Trotsky was murdered, Rivera feared for his own life as well. It seemed likely to him that Stalin would also want to kill the man who had sheltered the enemy. When Rivera was invited to paint another mural in San Francisco, he accepted on the spot.

This was Rivera's first mural commission in six years. It was arranged by the same man who had given him the work in the dining room at the San Francisco Stock Exchange. This time he was to paint a ten-paneled fresco on the theme of Pan-American unity. Rivera wanted to do a mural that combined what he viewed as the technical supremacy of North America with the creative brilliance of South America.[8]

Rivera worked on a scaffold that had been set up purposefully for optimal audience viewing, and huge crowds watched him paint daily.[9] One night Rivera was invited to dinner by Charlie Chaplin. The comic film actor made a deep impression on Rivera, who then added Chaplin to the mural.

In September, Rivera learned that Frida Kahlo was very ill. He sent for her to join him in California, where he believed the doctors were better trained and equipped than in Mexico. A doctor in San Francisco suggested to Rivera that more than anything else, Kahlo suffered from being separated from Rivera.[10] Despite their divorce, Rivera had never stopped loving Kahlo. Twice in the next two months, he asked her to marry him again. Twice she said no. The third time Rivera asked, Kahlo accepted.

A Return to Mexico

In a ceremony that took place on Rivera's fifty-fourth birthday, December 8, 1940, the artists remarried.

They went back to Mexico as soon as Rivera finished the Pan-American mural. Once there, Kahlo moved from their shared house back to the *Casa Azul*, the home in which she had grown up. Kahlo felt she needed privacy and a degree of independence from Rivera. She tiled the house in bright blues and yellows and whitewashed the walls and ceilings. Animals had free run of the place. One visitor reported, "There were monkeys jumping through the window at lunchtime. They just jumped up on the table, took some food and left. And there were seven hairless dogs."[11]

Kahlo's childhood home, *Casa Azul*, was where she felt happiest. Although she needed Rivera, she cherished living on her own.

A Museum of His Own

Diego Rivera called his museum Anahuacalli, after the area of Mexico where the Aztecs had lived before the Spaniards' arrival. Rivera drew the architectural plans for the building himself, as well as doing some of the actual construction. During this period, World War II was devastating much of the globe. The museum's construction site became a refuge for Rivera and Kahlo. He wrote later, "So while the bombs menaced our very lives and made painting seem a thing of insignificance, Frida and I started a strange kind of ranch. Here we planned to raise our own food staples, milk, honey, and vegetables, while we prepared to build our museum."[12]

Rivera was busy with a new house too. For more than twenty years, he had been collecting sculpture made by Mexican artists who had lived before the Spanish conquest of 1492. This art was called pre-Columbian or pre-Conquest. He had spent a lot of his money on this art—his friend Bertram Wolfe claimed it was "every spare peso"—and now he would spend a lot more building a museum for it.[13]

That Rivera needed a place to house the art was without question; his collection amounted to a staggering sixty thousand pieces of sculpture, the largest of its kind in Mexico.[14] What he ended up creating was a spectacular building carved from black volcanic lava stone. The structure resembles a great Aztec temple, complete with a moat and sacrificial altars just for show.

Inside, Rivera painted intensely colored frescoes with pictures of Aztec culture.

The pre-Conquest sculptures are displayed in many small interior rooms on the first floor, while the upper sections of the building were left as studio space for Rivera and Kahlo. The roof opened to a patio with views of Mexico City in the distance.

Rivera would continue working on his museum on and off, as his income permitted, for the rest of his life. With his typical bravado, he made plans to bequeath it to the Mexican government, but all arrangements were to be on his terms: "I shall dynamite the building with my own hands rather than have it put to some stupid use at odds with the purpose for which I designed it."[15] At nearly sixty years old, Diego Rivera was still a force to be reckoned with.

Diego Rivera: Mexican Muralist

This detail from *Dream of a Sunday Afternoon in Alameda Park* depicts Rivera, Kahlo, a skeleton, and printer José Guadalupe Posada.

Chapter 9

LATER WORKS

Rivera was commissioned to paint another mural in 1947, at the age of sixty-one. This mural would decorate the restaurant of the Hotel del Prado, a new hotel in Mexico City. Rivera made sure that, for restaurant patrons, the art would be a completely immersive experience. Measuring fifty feet long and sixteen feet high, the enormous fresco covered every bit of wall space.

Dream of a Sunday Afternoon in Alameda Park

Rivera called this mural *Dream of a Sunday Afternoon in Alameda Park*. Alameda Park is a leafy oasis in the center of Mexico City. It has immense old trees, stone fountains, and colorful flower gardens. For more than four hundred years, it has been a popular gathering place for Mexicans.

Rivera called his painting a dream because he brings together important historical figures with people who were important to him personally. Many of the historical figures actually lived in different centuries. In the mural, they stand side-by-side with friends and family of Rivera, posed as if for a group photograph, in what could only be a dream sequence.

At the very center of the group, Rivera painted himself as a child dressed in Sunday finery. Young Diego is in short pants, with a frog in one pocket and a snake in the other. A skeleton in a big hat holds his hand while Frida Kahlo hovers protectively behind. José Guadalupe Posada, the cartoonist and early influence on Rivera, stands on the other side of the skeleton.

Rivera weaves together the people who had the greatest professional and personal impact on his life. Mexican presidents are placed alongside artists. Minister of Education José Vasconcelos stands near Rivera's first wife, Lupe Marín. The Revolutionary war hero Emiliano Zapata rides his horse past Rivera's aunt Vicenta, who forced him to go to church when he was very young.

Everyday Mexican citizens play a large role in the painting as well. One man sells balloons, while another hawks newspapers, and another picks the pocket of a well-dressed gentleman. Fruit and tortilla vendors clash with the police, while children and their dogs frolic nearby.

Rivera Retrospective

When the mural was finished, as was so often the case with Rivera, a controversy ensued. Rivera had included in his group of significant historical figures Ignacio

Later Works

Calaveras

The skeleton standing near the center of *Dream of a Sunday Afternoon in Alameda Park* is known as a calavera in Spanish. Calaveras are symbols of the traditional "Day of the Dead," a holiday in which Mexicans honor their deceased ancestors. It is no coincidence that Rivera painted José Guadalupe Posada directly next to the skeleton. The nineteenth-century cartoonist was famous for using the calavera in his engravings.

Ramírez, a nineteenth-century scholar who had declared in a lecture that "God does not exist." Rivera not only painted Ramírez but had him holding a scroll on which his infamous words were written.

The archbishop of Mexico would not bless the hotel unless Rivera removed the offending text. Rivera refused. Then some Catholic students scratched out the words on the frescoed wall. The church and the vandals won out: The Hotel del Prado kept the mural hidden behind a red curtain.

Despite the conflict that engulfed it, *Dream of a Sunday Afternoon in Alameda Park* is generally considered by art historians to be one of the finest of Rivera's murals. Its success lies in the artist's skills at storytelling almost as much as in his skill at painting.

While the church continued to find fault with Rivera's art, the art community decided to officially praise

Dream's creator. In May 1949, the National Institute of Fine Arts opened a fifty-year retrospective of Rivera's work. Private collectors and museums from all over the world lent their Rivera paintings for the show. The exhibition was a great success.[1]

Another Mural Offends

The Mexican government then determined that it would be smart politics to send the whole show to Paris. It was high time, Mexican officials believed, that the world became more aware of the great artistic talent native to Mexico.

Rivera was commissioned to paint a new mural for the French exhibition. He was told that he could choose any theme that he wished. Rivera worked on his painting in secret. When the president of Mexico asked what he had decided upon, Rivera answered only, "I am painting a mural which will be dedicated to peace."[2]

When Rivera unveiled his mural, no one in the government was pleased. In yet another attempt to curry favor with the Communist Party, Rivera had painted a giant portrait of the Russian dictator Joseph Stalin. Next to Stalin, and almost as large, he had portrayed the Chinese Communist ruler Mao Tse-tung. To make matters worse, Rivera added a third image: Uncle Sam, symbol of the United States, armed with a machine gun.

After failing to convince Rivera to paint another mural that would not offend its American ally and at the same time would represent Mexico, not Communism, the Mexican government withdrew the funding for the

LATER WORKS

Paris exhibition. Rivera's one-man show would not cross the Atlantic. Further, the Communist Party made no move to readmit him.

Rivera's Communist-inspired mural did not go unnoticed in the United States. Some people argued that the murals he painted in Detroit should be demolished. The Detroit Art Commission responded to the protestors with this report:

> *We regret that Rivera's present behavior has revived the old controversy. There is no question that Rivera enjoys making trouble. . . . But this man, who often behaves like a child, is one of the outstanding talents of the Western Hemisphere. . . . In the Detroit frescoes we have one of the best as well as one of the most serious of his works. No other artist in the world could have painted murals of such magnitude and force. . . . We recommend that the paintings remain on exhibition.*[3]

A Funeral Turns Political

While Rivera was fighting with the government, Kahlo was fighting for her life. Though never good, her health took a rapid downturn after a failed operation on her spine. The next few years were especially difficult ones for her. But she continued to paint and in 1953 was given her first solo exhibition in Mexico.

Later that same year, Kahlo's right leg had to be amputated. Eleven months later, she died at only forty-seven years old. Because of her long history of medical problems, Rivera was not surprised by Kahlo's death, but he was deeply saddened. "July 13, 1954, was the most

Diego Rivera: Mexican Muralist

Although their artistic styles were quite different, and their long love affair endured much hurt and suffering, Frida Kahlo and Diego Rivera will be forever linked.

Later Works

tragic day of my life," he wrote afterward. "I had lost my beloved Frida forever."[4]

Kahlo's funeral service was to be held at the National Institute of Fine Arts, the same museum that had put together the retrospective for Rivera. The head of the museum was a longtime friend who wanted to honor Kahlo as an artist.

Rivera did not allow his grief for Kahlo to overshadow practical considerations. He decided to use Kahlo's funeral as an appeal for his re-entry to the Communist Party. In front of the many important Mexican government officials in attendance, he draped the coffin with a red and gold Communist flag. The newspaper account the following day read, "The funeral orations were not so much in honor of the dead artist as in praise of Communist ideas."[5]

The museum director was held responsible for Rivera's misbehavior and fired from his job. But after many years of trying, Rivera finally got what he wanted. Two months later, he was readmitted to the Mexican Communist Party.

Final Years

The next year, 1955, Rivera remarried. His new wife was an old friend and his art dealer, Emma Hurtado. Soon after the wedding, Rivera was diagnosed with cancer. He and Hurtado flew to the Soviet Union for medical treatment that was not available in Mexico.

Upon his return, Rivera decided that it was time to bring down the red curtain that had been concealing

Diego Rivera: Mexican Muralist

This is a front view of Diego Rivera's tomb. Mexico's most influential artists, politicians, war heroes, and intellectuals are in this cemetery.

Later Works

Dream of a Sunday Afternoon in Alameda Park for nine years. Calling the newspapers with the scoop that something important was about to occur at the Hotel del Prado, Rivera had a temporary scaffold put up in front of the mural. When the reporters had gathered, he ceremoniously climbed a ladder to paint over the words that had so angered the Catholic Church: "God does not exist." Then, to all present, Rivera, who had previously renounced religion, made the startling announcement, "I am a Catholic."[6] In Mexico, where nine of ten people are Catholic, Rivera's words and action were well received. At the Hotel del Prado, his mural was once again made available to public view.

On November 24, 1957, Rivera died at age seventy-one. Though Rivera had asked in his will to be buried next to Frida Kahlo at her childhood home, the president of Mexico instead ordered his body to be placed in the Rotunda of Illustrious Men at the Civil Pantheon of Dolores Cemetery in Mexico City, the place where many of the most important Mexicans have been buried.

Diego Rivera: Mexican Muralist

Diego Rivera used his artistic ability to comment on the politics of his time, as in this painting, *Mussolini* (1933).

108

Chapter 10

DIEGO RIVERA'S LEGACY

In Mexico, Diego Rivera is considered a great revolutionary. It is true that he did not fight alongside his countrymen in the bloody battles of the Mexican Revolution. But he used his art to celebrate and educate. Rivera championed the ideals of the Mexican Revolution in murals available to the public. His works celebrate the indigenous peoples of Mexico and criticize the abuses of power in the government and church.

In his art, Rivera aimed to give everlasting fame to the poor. For him, the humblest, least-educated citizen was as important as the wealthiest and most accomplished. In his paintings, presidents and generals hold equal rank with farmers and miners. To Rivera, each played a role of equal importance in Mexican society.

Rivera painted on walls in public spaces because he believed that art must be made available to all people. A mural on a public building could be seen for free by those for whom the cost of admission to a museum was a hardship and the price of a painting was forever beyond reach.

Many of these same citizens could neither read nor write. Rivera's murals provided a chronicle of Mexican history in pictures. For a government unable to provide classrooms for every child in Mexico, murals provided a crucial education.

The buildings Rivera painted were the most important buildings in Mexico. When government officials asked Rivera and others to paint the walls of the National Palace, the National School of Agriculture, or the Ministry of Education, they showed the public how much they valued this art as education.

When Rivera made art depicting everyday Mexicans struggling and succeeding, he helped to foster a feeling of national pride. His work brought solidarity and self-respect to a group of people long used to feeling put down. In vibrant colors and larger-than-life images, Rivera's murals speak boldly to all Mexicans.

Rivera left his mark in the United States as well. His frescoes in Detroit are among the best he ever did. Henry Ford may have invented the assembly line, but Rivera made it look beautiful. Because he believed that machines would free the worker from drudgery, Rivera painted men and machinery meshing in perfect rhythm.

As a man, Rivera did few things in perfect rhythm. He was often horribly selfish and hurtful to the women who loved him. Yet again and again, they forgave him.

Diego Rivera's Legacy

The women in his life seemed to have understood that for Rivera, art came before everything.

Many years after he left her, his first wife, Angelina Beloff, wrote, "He has never been a vicious man, but simply an amoral one. His painting is all he has ever lived for and deeply loved. And to his art, he has given the fidelity he could never find within him to give to a woman."[1]

Marevna Vorobev, the woman with whom Rivera had an affair and fathered a child, echoed this view, saying, "Perhaps it is wrong to judge him as a man, for he was an artist before anything else. All questions of conscience and duty came a distant second to his painting."[2]

And Frida Kahlo, the great love of Rivera's life, the woman who knew him best, was aware that his art came before her. "To Diego painting is everything. He prefers his work to anything else in the world. It is his vocation and his vacation in one."[3]

For his part, Rivera made no apologies about the fact that art was his first priority: "All I could say was that the most joyous moments of my life were those I had spent in painting."[4] While his devotion to his work made things difficult for those involved personally with him, the rest of the world has certainly benefited. Rivera's many murals and canvases have become a vital part of the world's impression of Mexico.

Rivera's life took many contradictory paths. He was a classically-trained painter who turned first to cubism, and then to muralism. As the leader of the Mexican

DIEGO RIVERA: MEXICAN MURALIST

This detail from the mural in the National Palace of Mexico features Frida among the masses. As a Communist, Rivera believed Mexicans from all stations in life should be celebrated.

DIEGO RIVERA'S LEGACY

Muralists, he was a Communist who took commissions from the wealthiest U.S. businessmen.

Rivera had tremendous energy and talent. He was a painter who loved his country and portrayed all Mexicans with the same dignity. In a creative career that spanned almost sixty years, Diego Rivera left a legacy of work supreme in the mural movement and equal to any of the twentieth century's finest artists.

Chronology

1886—Diego Rivera is born on December 8, 1886, in Guanajuato, Mexico. His twin brother, Carlos, survives only eighteen months.

1891—Sister María is born.

1892—Family moves to Mexico City.

1897—Begins eight years of study at San Carlos Academy.

1906—Travels to Spain; meets Angelina Beloff; goes to London.

1909—Goes to Paris.

1910—Returns to Mexico; ten-year Mexican Revolution begins.

1911—Returns to Paris for seven years.

1913—Begins cubist period; starts friendship with Picasso.

1914—World War I begins.

1915—Paints cubist masterpiece *Zapatista Landscape*.

1917—Ends cubist period, and moves in a new artistic direction.

1918—World War I ends; Rivera studies in Italy.

1921—Returns permanently to Mexico; ends relationship with Beloff; travels to Yucatán Peninsula with José Vasconcelos.

CHRONOLOGY

1922—Father dies; paints first mural, *The Creation*; marries Lupe Marín; joins Communist Party.

1923—Begins murals for Ministry of Education building.

1926—Paints mural at National School of Agriculture in Chapingo; meets Frida Kahlo.

1927—Divorces Lupe Marín.

1928—Travels to Russia; completes Ministry of Education murals.

1929—Marries Frida Kahlo; receives commissions for National Palace and Palace of Cortés murals; expelled from Communist Party; assumes directorship of San Carlos.

1930—Travels to the United States for the first time; paints murals at California School of Fine Arts and San Francisco Stock Exchange.

1931—One-man show opens at Museum of Modern Art, New York City.

1932—Paints murals for Edsel Ford at Detroit Institute of Arts.

1933—Paints mural for Nelson Rockefeller at RCA Building, New York City.

1934—RCA Building mural demolished.

1935—Begins period of portrait painting; builds a house with a bridge to separate areas for himself and Frida Kahlo.

1936—Paints mural at Hotel Reforma.

1937—Shelters Russian fugitive Leon Trotsky and his wife in Kahlo's Blue House.

1939—Divorces Kahlo.

1940—Paints mural in San Francisco, *Pan-American Unity*; remarries Frida Kahlo.

1942—Begins building a museum to house his collection of pre-Columbian sculpture and artifacts.

1947—Paints *Dream of a Sunday Afternoon at Alameda Park* for Hotel del Prado.

1949—National Institute of Fine Arts opens fifty-year retrospective.

1950—Paints Communist-inspired mural for French exhibition.

1951—Completes National Palace murals.

1954—Frida Kahlo dies; Rivera readmitted to Communist Party.

1955—Marries art dealer Emma Hurtado; diagnosed with cancer.

1956—Modifies Hotel del Prado mural.

1957—Dies on November 24 of heart failure.

Chapter Notes

Chapter 1. A Controversial Mural
1. Patrick Marnham, *Dreaming With His Eyes Open: A Life of Diego Rivera* (Berkeley: University of California Press, 1998), p. 251.
2. Diego Rivera with Gladys March, *My Art, My Life* (New York: Citadel Press, 1960), p. 129.

Chapter 2. Diego Rivera's Early Years
1. Patrick Marnham, *Dreaming With His Eyes Open: A Life of Diego Rivera* (Berkeley: University of California Press, 1998), p. 19.
2. Pete Hamill, *Diego Rivera* (New York: Harry N. Abrams, Inc., 1999), p. 12.
3. Diego Rivera with Gladys March, *My Art, My Life* (New York: Citadel Press, 1960), p. 3.
4. Ibid., p. 5.
5. Marnham, p. 31.
6. Rivera with March, p. 10.
7. Ibid.
8. Ibid., p. 11.
9. Hamill, p. 25.
10. Rivera with March, p. 16.
11. Ibid., p. 18.
12. Marnham, pp. 46–47.

Chapter 3. Leaving Mexico for Europe
1. Desmond Rochfort, *Mexican Muralists: Orozco, Rivera, Siqueiros* (San Francisco: Chronicle Books, 1993), p. 19.

2. Diego Rivera with Gladys March, *My Art, My Life* (New York: Citadel Press, 1960), p. 25.
3. Ibid.
4. Ibid., p. 27.
5. Bertram D. Wolfe, *The Fabulous Life of Diego Rivera* (New York: Scarborough House, 1963), p. 47.
6. Rivera with March, p. 30.
7. Wolfe, p. 55.
8. Patrick Marnham, *Dreaming With His Eyes Open: A Life of Diego Rivera* (Berkeley: University of California Press, 1998), p. 69.
9. Rivera with March, p. 34.
10. Marnham, p. 69.
11. Ibid., p. 73.
12. Pete Hamill, *Diego Rivera* (New York: Harry N. Abrams, Inc., 1999), p. 39.
13. Marnham, p. 83.
14. Ibid., p. 81.
15. Hamill, p. 47.
16. Rivera with March, p. 58.

Chapter 4. Embracing Cubism

1. Diego Rivera with Gladys March, *My Art, My Life* (New York: The Citadel Press, 1960), p. 59.
2. Ibid., p. 58.
3. Patrick Marnham, *Dreaming With His Eyes Open: A Life of Diego Rivera* (Berkeley: University of California Press, 1998), p. 93.
4. Rivera with March, p. 59.
5. Ibid., p. 60.
6. Ibid., p. 61.

Chapter Notes

7. Ibid., p. 62.
8. Marnham, p. 105.
9. Marevna Vorobev, *Life With the Painters of LaRuche* (New York: Macmillan Publishing Co., Inc., 1972), p. 57.
10. Rivera with March, p. 65.
11. Pete Hamill, *Diego Rivera* (New York: Harry N. Abrams, Inc.), p. 64.
12. Ibid., p. 67.

Chapter 5. Rivera's First Murals

1. Diego Rivera with Gladys March, *My Art, My Life* (New York: The Citadel Press, 1960), p. 58.
2. Patrick Marnham, *Dreaming With His Eyes Open: A Life of Diego Rivera* (Berkeley: University of California Press, 1998), p. 150.
3. Rivera with March, p. 72.
4. Marnham, p. 161.
5. Rivera with March, p. 10.
6. Desmond Rochfort, *Mexican Muralists: Orozco, Rivera, Siqueiros* (San Francisco: Chronicle Books, 1993), p. 21.
7. Rivera with March, p. 74.
8. Pete Hamill, *Diego Rivera* (New York: Harry N. Abrams, Inc., 1999), p. 96.
9. Anthony W. Lee, *Painting on the Left: Diego Rivera, Radical Politics, and San Francisco's Public Murals* (Berkeley: University of California Press, 1999), p. 52.
10. Marnham, pp. 169–170.
11. Rivera with March, p. 81.

Chapter 6. Diego and Frida

1. Bertram D. Wolfe, *The Fabulous Life of Diego Rivera* (Chelsea, Mich.: Scarborough House, 1963), p. 179.
2. Ibid.
3. Patrick Marnham, *Dreaming With His Eyes Open: A Life of Diego Rivera* (Berkeley: University of California Press, 1998), p. 180.
4. Diego Rivera with Gladys March, *My Art, My Life* (New York: Citadel Press, 1960), p. 102.
5. Ibid., p. 104.
6. Ibid., p. 83.
7. Marnham, pp. 194–195.
8. Pete Hamill, *Diego Rivera* (New York: Harry N. Abrams, Inc., 1999), p. 134.
9. Rivera with March, p. 104.
10. Ibid., p. 75.
11. Wolfe, p. 247.
12. Rivera with March, p. 101.
13. Ibid., pp. 94–95.
14. Ibid., p. 99.
15. Marnham, p. 214.

Chapter 7. American Commissions

1. Bertram D. Wolfe, *The Fabulous Life of Diego Rivera* (Chelsea, Mich.: Scarborough House, 1963), pp. 280–281.
2. Anthony W. Lee, *Painting on the Left: Diego Rivera, Radical Politics, and San Francisco's Public Murals* (Berkeley: University of California Press, 1999), p. 57.
3. Diego Rivera with Gladys March, *My Art, My Life* (New York: Citadel Press, 1960), p. 106.

CHAPTER NOTES

4. Patrick Marnham, *Dreaming With His Eyes Open: A Life of Diego Rivera* (Berkeley: University of California Press, 1998), pp. 232–233.
5. Desmond Rochfort, *Mexican Muralists: Orozco, Rivera, Siqueiros* (San Francisco: Chronicle Books, 1993), p. 124.
6. Rivera with March, p. 109.
7. Ibid.
8. Pete Hamill, *Diego Rivera* (New York: Harry N. Abrams, Inc., 1999), p. 155.
9. Wolfe, p. 277.
10. Marnham, p. 244.
11. Wolfe, p. 308.
12. Marnham, p. 248.
13. Ibid., p. 258.

Chapter 8. A Return to Mexico

1. Patrick Marnham, *Dreaming With His Eyes Open: A Life of Diego Rivera* (Berkeley: University of California Press, 1998), p. 263.
2. Diego Rivera with Gladys March, *My Art, My Life* (New York: Citadel Press, 1960), p. 120.
3. Xavier Moyssen, "The Self-Portraits of Diego Rivera" in *Diego Rivera: A Retrospective*, Cynthia Helms Newman, ed. (New York: W.W. Norton & Co., 1986), p. 195.
4. Rivera with March, p. 188.
5. Marnham, p. 279.
6. Ibid., p. 281.
7. Ibid., p. 265.

8. Anthony W. Lee, *Painting On the Left: Diego Rivera, Radical Politics, and San Francisco's Public Murals* (Berkeley: University of California Press, 1999), p. 208.
9. Pete Hamill, *Diego Rivera* (New York: Harry N. Abrams, Inc., 1999), p. 194.
10. Rivera with March, p. 150.
11. Marnham, p. 305.
12. Rivera with March, p. 155.
13. Bertram D. Wolfe, *The Fabulous Life of Diego Rivera* (Chelsea, Mich.: Scarborough House, 1963), p. 373.
14. Marnham, p. 297.
15. Ibid., p. 157.

Chapter 9. Later Works

1. Bertram D. Wolfe, *The Fabulous Life of Diego Rivera* (Chelsea, Mich.: Scarborough House, 1963), p. 381.
2. Ibid., p. 386.
3. Ibid., p. 390.
4. Diego Rivera with Gladys March, *My Art, My Life* (New York: Citadel Press, 1960), p. 178.
5. Wolfe, p. 402.
6. Ibid., p. 409.

Chapter 10. Diego Rivera's Legacy

1. Diego Rivera with Gladys March, *My Art, My Life* (New York: Citadel Press, 1960), p. 185.
2. Marevna Vorobev, *Life with the Painters of LaRuche* (New York: Macmillan Publishing Co., 1974), p. 138.
3. Rivera with March, p. 188.
4. Ibid., p. 180.

Glossary

billy club—A baton used as a weapon by law enforcement.

capitalism—Economic system in which industry is controlled by private owners, not the state, for profit.

cientificos—Believers in positivism in Mexico who advised president Porfirio Diaz.

commission—To hire an artist to create a piece of work.

communism—Political and economic system in which property and industry are owned and controlled by the state.

cubism—Art movement of the early twentieth century that abandoned the concept of realism and traditional perspective in favor of a two-dimensional, geometric approach.

encaustic—Painting technique that uses pigment melted with wax.

fresco—Painting technique where artists paints on damp plaster so that the colors penetrate the plaster.

hacienda—Estate that includes a house.

mural—Painting done directly on a wall.

salon—Gathering of artists discussing and showcasing their work, or a gallery of collected artworks.

scaffold—A movable platform used by muralists.

Señor—Masculine title used in the Spanish language, as sir or mister.

Further Reading

Books

Anreus, Alejandro, editor. *Mexican Muralism*. Berkeley, Calif.: University of California Press, 2012.

Dickerman, Leah and Anna Indych-Lopez. *Diego Rivera: Murals for the Museum of Modern Art*. New York: The Museum of Modern Art, 2011.

Reef, Catherine. *Frida & Diego: Art Love Life*. Boston: Houghton Mifflin Harcourt, 2014.

Rivera, Diego, with Gladys March. *My Art, My Life*. New York: Citadel Press, 1960.

Rosenthal, Mark. *Diego Rivera & Frida Kahlo in Detroit*. Detroit: Detroit Institute of the Arts, 2015.

Tuer, Dot and Elliot King, editors. *Frida & Diego: Passion, Politics and Painting*. Toronto: Art Gallery of Ontario and Atlanta: High Museum of Art, 2013.

Web Sites

diegorivera.com

Visit the Virtual Diego Rivera Web Museum to read news and learn about current and upcoming exhibitions.

nga.gov/exhibitions/2004/rivera/intro.shtm

The National Gallery of Art's Web site on Diego Rivera's life and art.

Index

A
Adams, Ansel, 77
Allegory of California, 78
Anahuacalli museum, 96

B
Beloff, Angelina, 31, 33 37, 40–41, 43–44, 46–47, 49, 51–53, 111
Blanchard, María Gutiérrez, 29, 31
Bondone, Giotto di, 52
Braque, Georges, 40

C
Café Dome, 40
Café Rotonde, 39–40, 43–44
calaveras (skeletons), 101
California School of Fine Arts mural, 76, 78
capitalism, 10, 77
Casa Azul, 91–92, 95
Cézanne, Paul, 31, 47
Chagall, Marc, 40
Chapingo, Mexico, 67
Chaplin, Charlie, 94
Chicharro, Eduardo, 25, 29–30
Communism, 10, 59, 67, 102
Communist Party, 57–58, 68, 72–73, 91, 102–103, 105
Cortés, Hernando de, 70, 72
cubism, 40–41, 47, 49, 111

D
Da Vinci, Leonardo, 73
Della Francesca, Piero, 52
Democrat, The, 20
Detroit Industry, 81
Detroit Institute of Fine Arts murals, 83, 85, 103
Detroit, Michigan, 8, 81, 83, 85, 87, 103, 110
Diaz, Carmen Romera Rubio de, 34
Díaz, Porfirio, 27–28, 34–35, 53
Dream of a Sunday Afternoon in Alameda Park, 99–102, 107

E
encaustic technique, 57, 59
Engels, Friedrich, 59

F
Fauré, Elie, 52–53, 55
Ford, Edsel, 81, 83
Ford, Henry, 81, 110
Ford Motor Company, 8
fresco technique, 52, 59, 61–62, 68, 72, 76–78, 80–81, 83
Frozen Assets, 80

G
Gerstle, William, 76
Great Depression, 75, 80
Gris, Juan, 40

Guanajuato, Mexico, 17–18, 21–22
   mummy exhibit, 21
Guerrero, Xavier, 61

H

haciendas, 28
Hitler, Adolf, 84
Hotel del Prado, 99, 101, 107
Hotel Reforma mural, 87–88

I

Ingres, Jean-Auguste-Dominique, 23

K

Kahlo, Frida
   death, 103, 105, 107
   health problems, 64, 94, 103
   marriage, 68, 70, 91, 92, 94–95
   meets Rivera, 64, 66
   paintings, 64, 66, 68
   traveling, 73, 77–78, 80–81, 83–85, 92

L

Lenin, Vladimir, 10

M

Madrid, Spain, 25, 29, 31, 37, 44
Making of a Fresco, The, 78
Marín, Guadalupe, 55, 57, 89, 100
Marx, Karl, 59
Matisse, Henri, 81
Mayan civilization, 54–55
Mexican-American War, 76

Mexican Communist Party, 72–73, 105
Mexican Indians, 89, 91
Mexican Revolution, 34–35, 58, 72, 109
Mexico City, 21–22, 24, 27–28, 31, 57, 63, 67, 80, 83, 87–88, 97, 99
Ministry of Education Building mural, 58–59, 61–62, 64, 66–68, 110
Modigliani, Amedeo, 40
Mondrian, Piet, 40
Montparnasse, Paris, 37, 39, 44
Moody, Helen Wills, 77–78
Morrow, Dwight W., 70
muralist movement, 57–58, 111–113
Murillo, Gerardo (Dr. Atl), 24–25
Museum of Modern Art, New York, 13, 80–81
Mussolini, Benito, 84

N

National Institute of Fine Arts, 102, 105
National Palace mural, 70, 72, 78, 110
National Preparatory School mural, 55, 58, 64
National School of Agriculture mural, 66–68, 110
New York City, 7, 11, 47, 80–81, 85, 87, 92

INDEX

O
Obregón, Alvaro, 53
Orozco, José Clemente, 58, 84–85

P
Palace of Cortés mural, 70, 72
Pan-American mural, 94–95
Paris, France, 27, 30–31, 33, 37, 39–44, 52, 102–103
Parra, Felix, 23
Picasso, Pablo, 40–43, 46–47
Porfiriato, 27, 35
Posada, José Guadalupe, 24, 100–101
Positivistic Scientists, 35

R
Ramírez, Ignacio, 100–101
RCA Building mural (*Man at the Crossroads*), 7–8, 10, 11, 13, 88
Rebull, Santiago, 23
Rivera, Carlos (brother), 15, 17–18
Rivera, Diego
  and Communism, 10, 59, 67, 102–103
  and controversy, 7–8, 10–11, 13–14, 83, 85, 87–88, 100–103, 105
  art shows and exhibitions, 2, 5, 33–35, 47, 80, 102–103
  awards and honors, 24, 33, 76
  childhood, 14–15, 17–18, 20–24
  children, 46–47, 49, 51, 57, 111
  cubist work, 39–44, 46–47, 111
  death, 107
  easel painting, 29, 58, 88–89, 91, 111
  education, 20, 22–25, 29–31, 35
  friendship with Picasso, 40–43, 46–47
  health, 30, 35, 87, 105
  in France, 30–31, 33–35, 40
  in Italy, 52–53
  in London, 31, 80
  in Russia, 67
  in Spain, 25, 28–30, 34, 37, 44
  in United States, 7, 70, 73, 77, 81, 85, 89, 103, 110, 113
  interest in ancient Mexican art, 54–55
  interest in machinery, 20, 78, 81, 110
  marriage to Emma Hurtado, 105
  marriage to Frida Kahlo, 68, 70, 91–92, 94–95
  marriage to Guadalupe Marín, 55, 57
  Museum of Modern Art show, 13, 80–81
  part of "Big Three," 57–58
  physical appearance, 7, 22, 28, 35, 53, 61, 63, 68, 77–78, 83, 87
  relationship with Angelina Beloff, 31, 33, 37, 40–41, 42–43, 46–47, 49, 51–53, 111
  sculpture museum, 96–97

teaching art, 54, 67
Rivera, Don Diego (father), 17–18, 20, 22
Rivera, María (mother), 15, 17–18, 22, 43, 44
Rivera, María (sister), 18, 43
Rockefeller, John D., 7–8
Rockefeller, Nelson, 8, 10–11, 13, 85, 87
Rosenberg, Léonce, 46–47
Rotunda of Illustrious Men, 107

S

Salon des Indépendants, 33
San Carlos Academy of Fine Arts, 22–24, 34, 72–73
San Francisco, California, 8, 76–78, 80, 87, 94
San Francisco Stock Exchange mural, 8, 76–78, 94
Sanzio, Raphael, 52
Siqueiros, David Alfaro, 58, 84–85
Stalin, Joseph, 68, 91–92, 94, 102
Standard Oil Company, 7–8

T

Trotsky, Leon, 91–92, 94
Tse-tung, Mao, 102

V

Van Gogh, Vincent, 47
Vasconcelos, José, 53–55, 58–59, 62, 100
Velasco, José María, 23
Vorobev, Marevna, 51, 111

W

Wolfe, Bertram D., 63, 68, 96
World War I, 40, 43–44, 52
World War II, 96

Y

Yucatán Peninsula, 54–55

Z

Zapata, Emiliano, 46, 100
Zapatista Landscape, 44, 46

37 27

RECEIVED APR 2 1 2016